STEPHEN JONES' MASTERS OF HORROR SERIES

The Weird Tales Boys

H.P. Lovecraft, Robert E. Howard,
Clark Ashton Smith and "The Unique Magazine"

STEPHEN JONES

INTRODUCTION BY
RAMSEY CAMPBELL

DIP

Thanks to Peter and Nicky Crowther, Mike Smith,
Marie O'Regan, Ramsey Campbell, Val and Les Edwards
and Michael Marshall Smith.

A Stephen Jones Book for Drugstore Indian Press an imprint
of PS Publishing Ltd. First published in September 2023
to commemorate the 70th birthday of Stephen Jones
and the centenary of *Weird Tales*.

2 4 6 8 10 9 7 5 3 1

ISBN 978-1-78636-998-7 [trade paperback]

Design and Layout by Michael Smith
Printed and bound in England by TJ Books Ltd, Padstow, Cornwall

PS Publishing Ltd.
Grosvenor House, 1 New Road
Hornsea HU18 1PG, England

editor@pspublishing.co.uk   www.pspublishing.co.uk

MIX
Paper from
responsible sources
FSC
www.fsc.org   FSC® C013056

THE MUSIC OF ERICH ZANN
by H.P. Lovecraft

LIST OF ILLUSTRATIONS

WONDERS OF THE WEIRD

I STARTED TO read *Weird Tales* before I knew I did, though the magazine had already fastened on my imagination. I may have been no more than six years old—certainly very little—when I saw a copy of the November 1952 issue in the window of a general store on Southport's Seabank Road. The largely luminous green cover appeared to depict a terrified avian creature beset by hideously malformed skeletons, more of which were rising from the earth, or so I thought then. Perhaps it simply shows a vulture ogling cadavers it has stripped, but pre-teenage Campbell yearned for not just the magazine but the terrors the cover seemed to promise. Even the logo lodged in my brain like a seed, but my mother was having none of anything that looked like that publication did. Hardcover books were a more acceptable matter, and so I was allowed to borrow adult fiction from the local library on her tickets. Little did either of us realise that some of the contents came from Weird Tales: minor early Lovecraft in a few of August Derleth's science fiction anthologies, Clark Ashton Smith's 'The Metamorphosis of Earth'. Long before my teens I was developing a taste for the weird.

My tenth birthday granted me permission to buy magazines and coincided with a flood of remainders on sale—British editions of American titles knocked down to sixpence the copy by Thorpe & Porter, the distributors. Among the many delights that claimed my pocket money was my first encounter with Robert E. Howard, his Lovecraft-related tale 'The Black Stone'. Soon I benefited from another kind of flood, Les of that name, whose Fantasy Book Centre in Bloomsbury advertised back issues of *Weird Tales* in that magazine. His postal service introduced me to the delights of collecting pulps. While Steve Jones for one has outstripped me for assiduousness, I still know that special pleasure of snagging yet another magazine that smells of all its years but, if we're lucky, appears to have clung to its youth. In some ways happening upon such an item unremarked and perhaps unappreciated in an ordinary bookshop or other second-hand emporium was best of all.

As I amassed my collection of *Weird Tales* and its competitors, not to mention publications that drew on it for material (the Boltonian *Phantom*, for instance), there were authors I increasingly hoped to find within. Out in front was Lovecraft, whose contributions I devoured, however minor (including a reprint of the body of 'The Poe-et's Nightmare', shorn of its satirical framing verses and hence transformed into a serious specimen of Lovecraftiana, entitled 'Alethia Phrikodes'). Soon Smith joined him in my personal pantheon of the weird, on the basis of stories such as 'The Double Shadow' and 'The Colossus of Ylourgne'. Howard took a place in it more gradually, perhaps because the haphazardness of collecting meant I read his tales of Conan out of sequence. There were other splendid writers—C.L. Moore, Frank Belknap Long, Margaret St. Clair, Manly Wade Wellman—but that trio seemed to sum up all that was best about *Weird Tales*.

Each of them was crucial to advancing their individual field. Besides uniting the British and American traditions of the tale of terror, Lovecraft progressively crossbred occult horror with science fiction to create a vital hybrid. Indeed, he devoted his career to trying out all the forms of the weird tale he could encompass and developing them further. His best work remains unsurpassed in care for structure and modulation of language. Smith's literary roots were in poetry, especially the decadents, and he drew upon this background to produce a body of fiction unrivalled for poetic morbidity, a rich concoction to be savoured by the connoisseur. Howard was the father and epitome of sword and sorcery, the most important contribution he made to fantasy during his incandescent career. His output remains astonishing, generated by the energy that powers much of his work. He was the youngest of the three to die, followed all too soon and young by Lovecraft. While Smith outlived them by decades, his productivity scarcely did. Perhaps they all needed that circumscribed time to achieve their creative concentration.

Now Steve Jones has celebrated them and the magazine—along with the publisher (Arkham House) that did so much to give them permanence, and their posthumous literary careers and influence—as only an aficionado can. While the details of their lives are often sobering, their imaginations rose above them and live on. Their literary descendants are roll-called too, and the multitudinous adaptations of the triumvirate's work. Drawing on a horde of sources, Steve's book corrects a few persistent misconceptions and draws our attention—certainly mine—to many media manifestations I for one never knew existed. It may well send you on a quest for some of them, and then the rest. After all, it's the work of a lifelong collector, and few activities are more infectious than collecting. May he continue to collect and write!

Ramsey Campbell
Wallasey, Merseyside
April 5, 2023

Dedicated to the memory of
ROBERT "BOB" WEINBERG
"Mr. *Weird Tales*"

WEIRD TALES

Printed in U. S. A.   THE UNIQUE MAGAZINE

MARCH, 1923   25 Cents

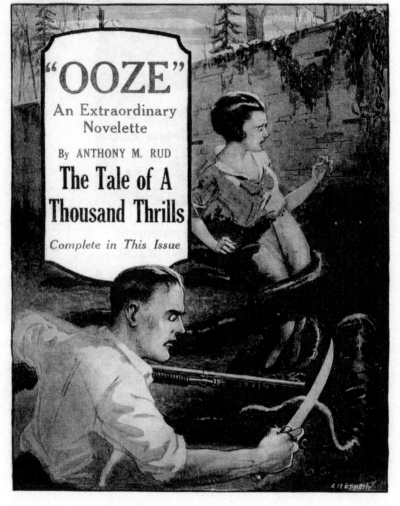

"OOZE"

An Extraordinary Novelette

By ANTHONY M. RUD

The Tale of A Thousand Thrills

Complete in This Issue

I

"It is the mission of Weird Tales to find present day writers who have this faculty, that our readers may glimpse the future—may be vouchsafed visions of the wonders that are to come."

—Otis Adelbert Kline

W HEN THE HISTORY of fantasy and horror fiction is being discussed, the pulp magazine *Weird Tales* is inevitably mentioned. Originally selling for just twenty-five cents on newsstands, and printed on low-grade "pulp" paper, *Weird Tales* was the first magazine devoted exclusively to weird and fantastic fiction. It ran for 279 issues, starting in March 1923 and finally giving up the ghost in September 1954. Although just one title amongst many hundreds being published at that time, it carried the subtitle "The Unique Magazine", and during its original thirty-two years run (the title has been revived on several occasions since with varied success) the Chicago-based magazine featured all types of fantasy fiction: from supernatural horror to sword and sorcery and even science fiction.

Under its second editor, Farnsworth Wright, *Weird Tales* began to flourish after years of financial problems, and some of its most famous contributors included Ray Bradbury, Robert Bloch, Richard Matheson, Seabury Quinn, Theodore Sturgeon, C.L. Moore, Henry Kuttner, Manly Wade Wellman, Jack Williamson, Henry S. Whitehead and even Tennessee Williams, to name just a few.

However, the three most important and influential writers to have their work published in the pages of "The Unique Magazine" were Rhode Island horror writer H.P. Lovecraft; the Texan creator of Conan the Cimmerian, Robert E. Howard; and the California poet, short story writer, illustrator and sculptor, Clark Ashton Smith.

This is their story.

In the early years of the 20th century, the American tradition of macabre fiction rested upon the shoulders of three writers—Edgar Allan Poe, Nathaniel Hawthorne and Ambrose Bierce. Although authors such as Henry James, Robert W. Chambers, Edith Wharton, Mary E. Wilkins-Freeman and a handful of others occasionally dabbled in the supernatural, at the time they were primarily associated with writing outside the genre.

It was not until the co-founding, in March 1923, of *Weird Tales* by publishers Jacob Clark Henneberger and John Marcus Lansinger that a new generation of writers would establish themselves, initially in the pages of "The Unique Magazine".

For the first year, under the editorship of mystery author Edwin F. Baird, *Weird Tales* floundered through a series of different formats, publication frequency and cover price, and was hopelessly in debt. The magazine's first anniversary was about to be marked by imminent bankruptcy, despite attempts by Henneberger to bring on board world-famous magician and escapologist Harry Houdini (Enrich Weiss) to boost circulation.

Author Otis Adelbert Kline stepped in to edit the triple-sized, first anniversary edition (May–July, 1924), and he anonymously penned a two-page manifesto entitled 'Why Weird Tales?' in which he explained:

Writers of highly imaginative fiction have, in times past, drawn back the veil of centuries, allowing their readers to look at the wonders of the present. True, these visions were often distorted, as by a mirror with a curved surface, but just as truly were they actual reflections of the present. It is the mission of *Weird Tales* to find present day writers who have this faculty, that our readers may glimpse the future— may be vouchsafed visions of the wonders that are to come.

In early 1924, Baird started to be edged out of his role with *Weird Tales*, and music critic and editorial assistant Farnsworth Wright was brought in as interim editor. By the time Wright officially took over at the helm of the title in the summer of 1925, he had negotiated a new deal that would enable him to obtain a major interest in the publication once the debts were paid off.

In late 1926, contributor E. Hoffman Price, who had made his debut in "The Unique Magazine" with his story 'The Prophet's Grandchildren' in the October 1925 issue, visited Wright in his office and recalled: "He was tall, very tall, and somewhat stooped; a large-framed, long-legged man, conspicuously and prematurely bald. My first impression was that his face gave no suggestion of his wit and sparkle. Neither did his voice, which was on the subdued rather than on the hearty side, but his eyes had a twinkle, keen and blue, and friendly."

Farnsworth Wright began to attract a new group of writers to the pages of *Weird Tales*. These youthful discoveries, many of whom would provide the bulk of the magazine's fiction throughout its precarious existence, included such names as Robert E. Howard, August W. Derleth, Frank Belknap Long, Jr., Edmond Hamilton, C.L. Moore, Henry Kuttner, Robert Bloch, Donald Wandrei and E. Hoffman Price. Other, already established, writers such as Clark Ashton Smith, Seabury Quinn and Henry S. Whitehead reached new peaks of popularity after Wright began publishing their work.

Of this latter group, perhaps the most important and influential contributor to the pulp magazine was H.P. Lovecraft.

II

"To me all mankind seems too local and transitory an
incident in the cosmos to take at all seriously."
—H.P. Lovecraft

HOWARD PHILLIPS LOVECRAFT was born on August
20, 1890, in his grandparents' home in Providence, Rhode
Island.

While he was still an infant, Lovecraft's family moved to
various locations in Massachusetts, never settling down for long.
Then in 1893 his father, travelling salesman Winfield Scott Lovecraft, apparently had a nervous breakdown while alone in a hotel
room and was committed to an insane asylum. Lovecraft's mother,
Sarah Susan (Phillips) Lovecraft, returned from Massachusetts
with her nearly three-year-old son to live in her parents' home.
Winfield Lovecraft died five years later, aged just forty-four, of
tertiary neurosyphilis.

As a child, Lovecraft led a somewhat sheltered early life,
coddled and pampered by his mother and her indulgent family.
Because his health was uncertain, his semi-invalidism (a nervous
disorder apparently exacerbated by his mother's own neurotic
obsessions) enabled him to read a great deal. Perhaps due to his
family's paternal English ancestry, his literary influences were the
"Gothics" of Mrs. Anne Radcliffe, Matthew Gregory Lewis and

Charles Maturin and such contemporary British authors as Arthur Machen and Lord Dunsany.

"Somehow I acquired a fondness for the past as compared to the present," Lovecraft recalled in 1924 in a letter to Henneberger; "a fondness which has plenty of chance to reign because of my semi-invalidism continued and kept me from college and business despite the most extravagant ambitions of boyhood."

In later years, the author liked to refer to himself in letters in the persona of an aged recluse, "Grandpa Theobald", and he affected the grammar and spelling of an 18th-century English gentleman, often ending a letter "Yr. Obt. Servt., HPL".

Something of a child prodigy, Lovecraft was taken out of school by his mother and taught at home by family members and private tutors. It was around this time, at the age of eight, that he discovered the work of a one-time fellow Providence resident, Edgar Allan Poe.

Poe would remain a life-long influence upon Lovecraft's writing, and the latter began experimenting with his own short tales of mystery and adventure.

According to his friend and protégé August Derleth, except for some minor juvenilia written when he was around six years old, Lovecraft preserved only a few of his early stories, most of which were written when he was between the ages of fifteen and twenty.

Despite the promise of such early tales as 'The Beast in the Cave' (1905), 'The Picture' (1907) and 'The Alchemist' (1908), Lovecraft was discouraged in his late teens, and he abandoned writing fiction for almost a decade. "It is only to be speculated about," mused Derleth, "whether that early promise would have been fulfilled sooner had Lovecraft's fiction then earned the encouragement it merited."

Several of the author's early stories and fragments were attempts to set down vivid dreams, apparently with the intention of expanding them into longer works later. The key to some of these dream sources can be found in Lovecraft's letters.

"Occasionally—but not often—a dream of mine forms a usable fictional plot," the author later revealed.

Physically, Lovecraft was a tall, thin, pale man, with bright eyes and a protruding jaw. Probably as a result of having near-photographic memory, he apparently utilised a wide vocabulary with a range that was revealed in his conversation and his writing.

"HPL carried himself with sufficient of a slouch to make me underestimate his height as well as the breadth of his shoulders," later recalled his friend and correspondent E. Hoffman Price, who first met Lovecraft in June 1932. "His face was narrow, longish, with long chin and jaw. His stride was brisk. His speech was quick, and inclined to jerkiness. It was as though his body was hard put to keep up with the agility of his mind, his eagerness to express his feelings."

Although he enjoyed cheese, chocolate, ice cream and sweet coffee, Lovecraft could not endure the cold and had a life-long aversion to sea food, as he explained to correspondent Donald Wandrei: "The very sight and smell of it nauseate me...one mouthful would make me actually and violently ill."

However, he was inordinately fond of cats and also keenly interested in astronomy and 18th-century architecture.

"He knew the year each house was built, who built it, who lived in it, every detail of its architecture and interior," recalled Wandrei about a walking tour of Providence he undertook with Lovecraft. "He was a pure antiquarian of prodigious memory."

Much of Lovecraft's writing was done at night, in longhand with a fountain pen, often on the reverse of old letters and other papers. For much of his writing career he would destroy the original manuscripts as soon as they were published.

While in his early twenties, he became immersed with the amateur journalism movement. He also began contributing astronomical articles to local newspapers while expanding a growing circle of correspondence, often averaging eight to ten letters a day, each usually four to eight pages in length.

Despite having long maintained that he had no talent for fiction, around 1915 Lovecraft was urged to try his hand at writing short stories again. His macabre tale 'Dagon' (written in July, 1917) was published by his friend and fellow member of the United Amateur Press Association, W. Paul Cook, in the November 1919 issue of Cook's amateur journal, *The Vagrant*. It was followed three years later by 'The Tomb', which had been written a month before the earlier story, in the March issue of the same magazine.

Meanwhile, another tale, 'Polaris' (written circa May, 1918), had appeared in the December 1920 issue of Alfred Galpin's *The Philosopher*.

Although he received no payment for these stories, they provided Lovecraft with an opportunity to hone his craft as a writer of the supernatural.

Around 1918, Lovecraft had discovered that he could make a small amount of money by revising the work of his fellow amateur writers. In fact, for many years these (usually anonymous) revisions became Lovecraft's major source of income, with his own fiction merely a sideline.

"Since revision jobs are always irregular," Lovecraft explained in a letter to teenage correspondent Willis Conover, Jr., "with long gaps between, and so exhausting that one can't do them justice without a vast amount of time and energy, it follows that they aren't a very profitable source of income."

Although much of this work consisted of correcting spelling, punctuation and grammar, or copying out manuscript pages, he would sometimes entirely revise and rewrite a story if its content inspired his imagination.

This was the case with 'The Crawling Chaos', an early dream-narrative written in 1920–21 with the amateur poet Winifred

Virginia Jackson and published under the double pseudonyms "Lewis Theobold, Jr., and Elizabeth Neville Berkley" in the April 1921 issue of *The United Co-operative*, another amateur magazine.

Amongst the authors whose work he substantially rewrote or revised were United States consul Adolphe de Castro; family friend and fellow Providence resident C.M. Eddy, Jr.; writer and editor Wilfred Blanch Talman; Midwest journalist and romance writer Zealia B. Bishop; Massachusetts divorcée Hazel Heald; world traveller William Lumley; Lovecraft's future wife Sonia Greene, and even magician and escape artist Harry Houdini, all of whom went on to sell their fiction to *Weird Tales*.

"He would criticize paragraph after paragraph and pencil remarks beside them," recalled Hazel Heald, "and then make me rewrite them until they pleased him."

"As a writer and instructor in the field of supernatural fiction," Zealia Bishop remembered, "he was an undisputed master, and another's work seldom pleased him when he first saw it. He could always find much to improve, and he was generous with his advice, drawing on a vast store of knowledge quite beyond the capacity of the average man of education of his or our time."

From 1919 until 1929, Lovecraft himself produced a number of similar works that were probably influenced by his discovery of Lord Dunsany's books. Several of these stories featured the character of Randolph Carter, possibly intended as a fictional representation of the author himself. The first of these tales was the dream-inspired 'The Statement of Randolph Carter', written in December 1919 and published in May the following year in the thirteenth issue of Cook's *The Vagrant*.

Randolph Carter returned a further three times—in 'The Silver Key' (written in 1926), the posthumously published short novel 'The Dream-Quest of Unknown Kadath' (written between late 1926 and early 1927) and the collaboration with E. Hoffman Price, 'Through the Gates of the Silver Key' (written between October,

1932 and April, 1933). Price persuaded Lovecraft to revise and expand his 6,000-word first draft, and the 14,000-word result was published (after being initially rejected by Farnsworth Wright) in the July 1934 *Weird Tales*.

"Price liked my old story 'The Silver Key' (*Weird Tales*, January 1929) and urged me to write a sequel," Lovecraft revealed to Willis Conover. "I didn't feel like it, hence postponed the matter. Then Price wrote a sequel himself, and sent it to me to look over. I found it so different in spirit from the original story that I rewrote it extensively, and added a new part longer than Price's."

"When I deciphered his manuscript, I estimated that he had left unchanged fewer than fifty of my original words," Price later recalled.

A further attempt by Price to convince the author to collaborate on another Randolph Carter story in 1934 was rejected by Lovecraft, who claimed that it would be too much of a "strain".

"In the past I have allowed myself to be persuaded into a few collabor-ative ventures—to please the other guy—but the results have never been satisfactory," Lovecraft wrote to Conover. "Now I am compelled by sheer necessity to call a halt. I have more ideas of my own than I have time to develop, and what little time and energy I *can* spare must go into these."

Always an intensely nervous person, Lovecraft's mother "Susie" had been in a declining mental state for many years. At the age of sixty-two, she died in the same hospital for the insane as her husband on May 24, 1921. In letters to friends Lovecraft described the event as giving him "an extreme nervous shock" and recalled that "My mother was, in all probability, the only person who thoroughly understood me."

In his controversial 1975 volume, *Lovecraft: A Biography*, author L. Sprague de Camp came to a different conclusion: "He was a man who, as a result of congenital tendencies (his schizoid personality), compounded by an abnormal upbringing, was long delayed in maturation. He showed adolescent bumptiousness, prejudices, dogmatism and affectations, and adolescent timidity towards new human contacts and relationships, in his thirties, more than a decade after he had ceased to be an adolescent. In some respects, such as the sexual and the monetary, he never did mature."

With his mother's death, Lovecraft found himself being coddled by his two indulgent aunts, Lillian Phillips Clark and Annie Emeline Phillips Gamwell. They all lived together under the same roof for three years.

Lovecraft had always had women around to care for him. Although he was comfortable living with his aunts, it was only a matter of time before he began looking around for a bride. He didn't actually bother to look very far.

After first meeting her at a gathering of the National Amateur Press Association in Boston in 1921, Lovecraft married the Ukrainian-born Sonia Haft Greene, a woman seven years his senior, in St. Paul's Church, New York, on March 3, 1924. "He said nothing could please him better," she noted some years later.

The newlyweds lived together in south Brooklyn, while Sonia worked for a fashionable woman's wear establishment on Manhattan's Fifth Avenue. However, within less than two years the marriage was in trouble, with Lovecraft moving back to Rhode Island and the couple basically living separate lives.

"I believe he loved me as much as it was possible for a temperament like his to love," wrote Sonia. "I had hoped . . . that my embrace would make of him not only a great genius but also a lover and husband. While the genius developed and broke through the chrysalis, the lover and husband receded into the background until they were apparitions that finally vanished."

"There was a general feeling that the marriage was not destined to last, nor did it," observed the author's friend, critic Rheinhart Kleiner.

Sonia (who had married once before, when she was sixteen)

eventually urged Lovecraft to divorce her and, on March 25, 1929, he signed a preliminary decree on the grounds of her "wilful desertion".

"I told him I had done everything I could think of to make our marriage a success," Sonia wrote, "but that no marriage could be such in letter-writing only."

The couple continued to correspond sporadically, and Sonia last saw her former husband in 1932. She eventually moved to California where, after three years, she married a former university professor. The marriage lasted until his death, a decade later.

A month after Lovecraft's death, the poet Samuel Loveman put a classified advert in *The New York Times* in an attempt to contact his friend's former wife, who had already heard the news from another source. "Even though I am not his widow," she wrote later, "I mourn in sorrow and reverence his untimely passing."

Sonia herself died on December 26, 1972 at the age of 89. Towards the end of her life, it was alleged that Lovecraft had apparently never executed the document required to make their divorce final. As a result, Sonia's third and final marriage was quite possibly bigamous.

"Despite all one may think of the bizarre affair of Lovecraft's marriage," recalled Kleiner some years later, "I am inclined to believe that the former Sonia Greene, however misguided or ill-advised, was sincere in her own way."

For the remainder of his life, Lovecraft made his home in his beloved Providence, where he remained a studious antiquarian. However, he was no hermit, and he managed to travel extensively as he eked out a precarious living.

"I have never had much inclination to depend on people for amusement," Lovecraft explained. "To me all mankind seems too local and transitory an incident in the cosmos to take at all seriously. I am more interested in scenes—landscapes and architecture—I have a very real affection for the old town with its ancient steeples and belfries, hills and corners, courts and lanes, all reminding me of that 18th century and that Old England which I love so well."

Weird Tales

THE UNIQUE MAGAZINE

IMPRISONED WITH
the **PHARAOHS**
by
HOUDINI
in this issue

ANNIVERSARY NUMBER 50c

**FIFTY DISTINCT FEATURE
NOVELS, SHORT STORIES
AND NOVELETTES.
THRILLS! MYSTERY!
ADVENTURE!**

III

"I pay no attention to the demands of commercial
writing. My object is such pleasure as I can obtain
from the creation of certain bizarre pictures,
situations, or atmospheric effects; and the only
reader I hold in mind is myself."

—H.P. Lovecraft

F OR A WRITER so influential, it is perhaps surprising to
realise that Lovecraft's major fiction output barely spanned
two decades.

Having co-founded the pulp magazine *Weird Tales* in 1923,
publisher J.C. Henneberger had apparently read Lovecraft's serials
'Grewsome Tales' (written 1921–22, and later retitled 'Herbert
West—Reanimator') and 'The Lurking Fear' (written in November
1922) in George Julian Houtain's professional humour magazine
Home Brew. Impressed by Lovecraft's work, Henneberger later
claimed that he eventually convinced the reluctant author, who still
considered writing to be no more than a gentlemanly hobby, to
send five manuscripts to editor Edwin Baird in May 1923.

However, as author John Locke revealed in his revisionist
history *The Things Incredible! The Secret Origins of Weird Tales*
(2018), Henneberger's faulty recollections don't actually correlate
with the facts. Much more likely was that Lovecraft discovered the
nationally distributed magazine on the newsstands and, at the
urging of several friends and despite his initial pessimism, decided
to submit some of his work to editor Baird.

In fact, Lovecraft sent Baird the manuscripts for five stories, four of which ('Dagon', 'The Statement of Randolph Carter', 'The Cats of Ulthar' and 'Facts Concerning the Late Arthur Jermyn and His Family') had already appeared in amateur journals. The fifth, previously unpublished story, was 'The Hound' (written in 1922).

"I have no idea that these things will be found suitable," explained the recalcitrant author in his covering letter, "for I pay no attention to the demands of commercial writing. My object is such pleasure as I can obtain from the creation of certain bizarre pictures, situations, or atmospheric effects; and the only reader I hold in mind is myself."

Lovecraft compounded his negativity by insisting that, should "any miracle" lead to Baird publishing any of the stories, the editor must agree that "If the tale cannot be printed as written, down to the very last semicolon and comma, it must gracefully accept rejection."

Despite Lovecraft's pessimistic tone, Baird bought all five of the tales—although not before he asked the author to retype them, double-spaced—and urged him to submit more. In the eleven issues of *Weird Tales* published from October 1923 to February 1925, Lovecraft appeared in eight of them with nine stories and a poem.

Lovecraft's initial run of fiction in "The Unique Magazine" comprised 'Dagon' (in the October, 1923 issue), 'The Picture in the House' (December 1923–January, 1924), 'The Hound' (February, 1924), 'The Rats in the Walls' (March, 1924), 'The White Ape' (a retitling of 'Facts Concerning the Late Arthur Jermyn and His Family') and the poem 'Nemesis' (both April, 1924), 'Hypnos' and the pseudonymous 'Imprisoned with the Pharaohs' (both May–July, 1924), 'The Festival' (January, 1925) and 'The Statement of Randolph Carter' (February, 1925). However, Lovecraft continued to balk at typing his own manuscripts and got C.M. Eddy to do it in return for doing revision work on his friend's stories.

According to author Frank Belknap Long, Jr., another close friend of the author, Baird's admiration for Lovecraft's fiction "verged upon idolatory [*sic*], and he clearly felt that if *Weird Tales* failed to contain three or four Lovecraft stories in the course of a year, there would ensue a reader disappointment of a very serious nature."

However, that did not stop Lovecraft writing to "Leetle Bairdie" in February 1924 to complain: "I was delighted to receive your two communications, and to hear that you like 'Nemesis'. This delight atones fairly well for the sensation of gastric depression caused by the implication that 'Arthur Jermyn' is going to press as 'The White Ape'! I wish I could convert you to my point of view regarding the annoying literalness and flaccidity of that later title."

That same year, the magazine found itself in serious financial problems. Baird was mostly sidelined as editor and, with the help of part-time assistants Farnsworth Wright and writer and future literary agent Otis Adelbert Kline, Henneberger took over the editorial reins to produce a bumper anniversary issue.

For this special edition, Henneberger commissioned Lovecraft to ghost write a story to be published under the by-line of world-renowned magician Harry Houdini. Houdini had previously been represented in the magazine with the two-part serial 'The Spirit Fakers of Hermannstadt' (March, 1924) and 'The Hoax of the Spirit Lover' (April, 1924), along with a short-lived column, 'Ask Houdini'.

It has been speculated that the first two Houdini stories may have actually been written by Walter Gibson, creator of pulp hero The Shadow and a magician himself. Other names that have been mentioned include Baird, Kline and Wright themselves, along with C.M. Eddy and another *Weird Tales* contributor, Harold Ward.

Written in February of that year under the title 'Under the Pyramids', Lovecraft's first-person narrative involved Houdini battling subterranean monstrosities beneath the Egyptian pyramids.

Giving himself the credit "Translated by H.P. Lovecraft", the author completed the manuscript shortly before he boarded a train at Union Station, Providence, on March 2, 1924 to travel to Manhattan to marry Sonia Greene. However, an understandably preoccupied Lovecraft lost the original typescript somewhere in the station, and he spent the following morning—his wedding day—retyping the manuscript from his notes. With the work only half-finished before he had to attend the ceremony, he used the following day and night of his honeymoon in Philadelphia to complete the job.

"I alone was able to read those crossed out notes," recalled Sonia. "I read them slowly to him while he pounded at a typewriter borrowed from the hotel... and when the manuscript was finished we were too tired and exhausted for honeymooning or anything else. But I wouldn't let Howard down, and the manuscript reached the publisher on time."

Such was his hope that it would revive the magazine's flagging fortunes, Henneberger paid Lovecraft $200 for the story, retitled it 'Imprisoned with the Pharaohs', and gave it the cover of his oversized "Anniversary Number" (May–July, 1924). Unfortunately, Lovecraft's promised by-line was left off the published version.

Houdini reportedly liked the story very much and, not only did he apparently invest money in the struggling publication, but Henneberger, Houdini and Lovecraft did meet up at least once in New York City to confer about future projects. Unfortunately, these and other discussions eventually came to nothing, and the fifty-two-year-old escape artist tragically died during a performance in Detroit on Halloween, 1926.

When Henneberger's subsequent attempts to convince Lovecraft to become the new editor of *Weird Tales* or a similar periodical devoted to ghost stories were reputedly rejected because it would involve a move to Chicago, Farnsworth Wright was finally appointed the new editor of *Weird Tales*. Under Wright's editorship, the magazine finally started to flourish after several years of financial uncertainty.

In a 1928 letter to Derleth, Lovecraft described Wright, who suffered from Parkinson's disease which became progressively worse during his years editing *Weird Tales*, as "an admirably amiable, conscientious & honourable person despite his limitations in critical judgment".

According to E. Hoffman Price, Wright once told him: "Often I buy a story because I like it. But always, I am obliged first to consider whether my readers would like that yarn. Many a time, I've accepted things which I did not care for, but which I felt would please many of the readers".

Wright rejected Lovecraft's new story 'The Shunned House' in 1924 because, at over 10,000 words, he thought it was too long and slow. He did, however, continue to buy such tales as 'The Statement of Randolph Carter' (for the February, 1925 issue), 'The Music of Erich Zann' (May, 1925), 'The Unnamable' (July, 1925), 'The Temple' (September, 1925), 'The Tomb' (January, 1926), 'The Cats of Ulthar' (February, 1926), 'The Outsider' (April, 1926), 'The Moon Bog' (June, 1926), 'The Terrible Old Man' (August, 1926), 'He' (September, 1926), 'The Horror at Red Hook' (January, 1927), 'The White Ship' (March 1927), 'Pickman's Model' (October 1927), 'The Lurking Fear' (January, 1928), 'The Call of Cthulhu' (February, 1928) and 'The Silver Key' (January, 1929). However, several of these stories had appeared previously in amateur publications.

"With *Weird Tales* as perhaps the only exemplar of this type of fiction," explained Robert Bloch, the author of *Psycho*, "Lovecraft's work exerted a very strong influence. The things he talked about were strange, were novel, were mysterious. The whole concept of a cosmology in which evil forces controlled the universe was very fresh, and some of his characters and characterizations were quite shocking.

"Today, when one reads Lovecraft, one reads him with echoes of countless science-fiction, television, and motion picture images in his or her mind. But at the time, I can assure you, most of the people I knew that had met the world of Lovecraft for the first time were quite frightened by it."

Following the appearance of 'The Dunwich Horror' in the April 1929 *Weird Tales* (for which the magazine paid $240.00—the most Lovecraft had received for a story up until that time), negative reaction to the tale's gruesomeness resulted in Wright not publishing any new fiction by the author again until 'The Very Old Folk' appeared in the February–March 1931 issue.

Wright had already rejected 'Cool Air' (written in March, 1926), even though Lovecraft considered it "not nearly so bad as many he has taken". The story ultimately appeared in the penultimate March 1928 issue of *Tales of Magic and Mystery*, a classy-looking but short-lived pulp that ran for just five issues. Wright eventually purchased the story after Lovecraft's death, and he used it in the September 1939 edition of *Weird Tales*.

Although he also initially turned down 'The Strange High House in the Mist' (written in November, 1926), Wright subsequently changed his mind and published it in the October 1931 issue for $55.00. He had also rejected 'In the Vault' (written in September, 1925) for being too gruesome, yet he finally bought it six years later for the magazine (after August Derleth persuaded Lovecraft to let him retype the "all but unreadable" manuscript) without any comment.

After selling another tale rejected by Wright, 'The Colour Out of Space', to Hugo Gernsback's archetypal science fiction magazine *Amazing Stories* in 1927—and receiving a paltry fifth of a cent of a word for it after having to write several letters demanding payment—Lovecraft refused to offer his fiction to any magazine except *Weird Tales*. However, he also resisted selling those stories turned down by Wright to other markets, even though many of them paid better rates: "I have a sort of dislike of sending in anything which has been once rejected," Lovecraft admitted.

This reluctance to re-submit his work even applied to the 42,000-word novelette 'At the Mountains of Madness', which Wright had rejected in June 1931. About an Antarctic expedition that stumbles upon an ancient city whose alien inhabitants are still alive, Lovecraft wrote in 1931: "'At the Mountains of Madness' has a certain kind of cumulative horror, but is altogether too slow for the cheap artificial markets."

Despite the author's doubts as to its suitability, the story was eventually agented by young Brooklyn fan (and later literary agent and renowned comic-book editor) Julius Schwartz to *Astounding Stories*, where editors F. Orlin Tremaine and Desmond Hall paid $350.00 for it. It was serialised in somewhat abridged form over three issues in February–April, 1936. Unfortunately, Schwartz's plans to sell a collection of Lovecraft's work to a British book publisher came to nothing.

Around the same time, Donald Wandrei also sold 'The Shadow Out of Time' (1934) for Lovecraft to *Astounding* for $280.00. (Wandrei later claimed to have also sold 'At the Mountains of Madness' to the magazine.) "The checks, amounting to many hundreds of dollars, rescued Lovecraft from a serious financial plight," he explained. However, despite earning more for his fiction than ever before, Lovecraft complained about Tremaine's editing of his manuscripts and considered them still unpublished.

Although he thought of himself as essentially a prose writer, Lovecraft also dabbled extensively in poetry. In the early 1930s he wrote a series of thirty-six weird sonnets in little more than a week. He sold ten to *Weird Tales* for $35.00 and others appeared in such fan publications as *The Fantasy Fan*, *Science-Fantasy Correspondent*, *The Phantagraph* and *The Acolyte*. The cycle was eventually collected under the title *Fungi from Yuggoth* in an amateur booklet published in an edition of less than 100 copies by William H. Evans of Eugene, Oregon, in 1943. It was later included, along with the ambitious werewolf poem 'Psychopompos' (written

1917–18) and other verse, in the 1963 Arkham House volume *Collected Poems*.

"Much of the poetry falls into two main categories," observed author and poet Joseph Payne Brennan, "deliberately archaic work imitative of 18th-century verse, and a group of weird sonnets known as 'Fungi from Yuggoth'. The imitative verse is interesting and often competent, but I think the 'Fungi' sonnets are far more arresting and effective."

Written over six months in late 1925 or early 1926, Lovecraft's influential 30,000-word essay 'Supernatural Horror in Literature' appeared in the only edition of W. Paul Cook's amateur journal *The Recluse* in the middle of 1927.

Following its initial printing, Lovecraft almost immediately began making notes to update his study, and a slightly revised version was serialised over seventeen instalments in Charles D. Hornig's fanzine *The Fantasy Fan* between October 1933 and February 1935. However, the essay remained incomplete when that periodical ceased publication.

According to British horror writer Ramsey Campbell: "Lovecraft's 'Supernatural Horror in Literature' is not only an appreciation of all that he found best in the genre and a critique of the flaws he saw, but also a statement of his own artistic ambitions."

"I think it is probably the finest piece of non-fiction which Lovecraft ever wrote," agreed Brennan.

During the late 1920s and early '30s, some of H.P. Lovecraft's stories began to be reprinted in hardcover anthologies. 'The Call of Cthulhu' appeared in *Beware After Dark!* (1929) edited by T. Everett Harré, and Dashiell Hammett included 'The Music of Erich Zann' in his *Creeps by Night* (1931) anthology. In Britain, Christine Campbell Thomson, editor of the *Not at Night* series published by Selwyn & Blount, Ltd., included 'The Horror at Red Hook' in *You'll Need a Night Light* (1927), 'Pickman's Model' in *By Daylight Only* (1928) and 'The Rats in the Walls' in *Switch on the Light* (1928).

'The Horror at Red Hook' additionally turned up in editor Herbert Asbury's pirated omnibus *Not at Night!* (1928) from New York's Macy-Masius/The Vanguard Press.

Equally obscure today, 'The Music of Erich Zann' was also reprinted in the "Great Short Stories" series in the October 24, 1932 edition of the *The London Evening Standard* newspaper.

Unfortunately, Lovecraft had not paid much attention to retaining the rights to his fiction, and consequently received little or nothing for these reprints and also others in *Weird Tales*.

He defended his attitude by exclaiming: "If this is 'poor business', then I say damn business!"

Lovecraft also kept up a voluminous correspondence with numerous people, including many of his fellow contributors to *Weird Tales*. These included his young protégés August W. Derleth and Frank Belknap Long, Jr.; Episcopal minister Henry S. Whitehead; Catherine L. Moore and her future husband Henry Kuttner; the youthful J. Vernon Shea; Fritz Leiber, Jr., the son of a famous Shakespearean actor, and Robert E. Howard, creator of Conan the barbarian.

"Lovecraft appears to have had an instinct for bringing together persons who would be congenial, each for the sake of the other, and not merely because each held HPL in such high esteem," observed E. Hoffman Price.

One fellow contributor to "The Unique Magazine" who he had regularly been writing to since 1922 was Californian poet and artist Clark Ashton Smith.

IV

"Let him who is worthy by reason of his clear eye
and unjaded heart wander across these borders of
beauty and mystery and be glad."
—Gerorge Sterling

C LARK ASHTON SMITH was born on Friday, January 13, 1893, in Long Valley, a Northern California town in the Sierra foothills not far from Auburn. In 1891, Smith's English-born father Timeus Smith married farmer's daughter Mary Frances ("Fanny") Gaylord, who was about four years older than he was. Clark was their only child.

Both of his parents were around forty when he was born, and Smith later claimed that he was descended from Norman-French counts and barons, of Lancashire baronets and Crusaders. One of his Ashton ancestors was apparently beheaded as part of Guy Fawkes' notorious Gunpowder Plot, while his mother's family— the Gaylords—were French Huguenots fleeing persecution, who arrived in New England in 1630.

In 1902 Timeus Smith bought a tract of arid volcanic hilltop known as "Indian Ridge" (later "Boulder Ridge"), in mining country, east of Sacramento. The forty-four-acre property was situated only six miles from the place of Clark's birth, about two miles from Old Town, Auburn, and a quarter of a mile from the highway and the nearest neighbours. There, Timeus dug a well and attempted to farm chickens while his wife sold magazine subscriptions.

Over the next five years, in a grove amongst the blue oak trees, Timeus constructed a dark, single-storey, four-room wooden frame house for his family.

"The cabin itself was old and small with a lean-to at the back and a broad sleeping porch extending the full length of the front" later recalled Clark Ashton Smith's friend George F. Haas. "The wide boards and wood shingles of the sides were silvered and grey; on the roof were dark tar-paper shingles." Smith himself later built a low stone wall across the front of the property, using lava and granite boulders he found laying on the ground nearby.

With little money to spare, the family had to be self-sufficient. Wood for cooking and heating came from the surrounding trees, kerosene lamps supplied light, and water was obtained from a natural underground spring, situated in a prospector's mine-shaft which also doubled as a cold storage, only a few feet from the cabin.

During the hot summers, Smith would work outside on a rickety homemade wooden table and he slept in a tattered sleeping bag spread over an old metal army cot.

Author E. Hoffman Price had the distinction of being the only correspondent to meet Lovecraft, Howard and Smith in person. After his first visit to the latter in April 1934, he recalled his impression that there were two Clark Ashton Smiths: "There was an old, old Smith, weary and not too steady, and a little stooped; grave and ancient of expression; high-keyed, sensitive, with a slight twitch near the corners of the mouth". However, he also observed, "a smiling, boyish Smith, with a twinkle in the eye, a glint as though he spent much of his time relishing the total silliness and absurdity of things, seeing through surface and substance and laughing at most of what he saw".

Except for five years in a grammar school, Smith was entirely home-educated after an early illness (possibly scarlet fever) cut short his formal learning. With a youthful appreciation of the *Arabian Nights* and the works of Edgar Allan Poe, he began writing at the age of eleven, and by the time he was seventeen he had sold four short Oriental tales to such popular magazines as *The Black Cat* and *The Overland Monthly*.

However, except for a single appearance in the August 1924 issue of *10 Story Book*, Smith's attempts at selling sophisticated romance stories met with repeated rejections. It was also during this period that Smith wrote an unpublished 90,000-word Arabian Nights novel entitled *The Black Diamonds*.

Smith's major literary influence in his teens was the baroque Romantic poetry of San Francisco bohemian and newspaper columnist George Sterling. A protégé of Ambrose Bierce and a close friend of novelist Jack London, Sterling worked in the tradition of Keats and Shelley. Although that style of florid verse had passed mostly out of vogue by the early 1900s, it remained popular in California into the early 1920s thanks to a remarkable group of poets now known as the "California Romantics", whose ranks included Sterling, Bierce and Nora May French.

Smith was particularly influenced by Sterling's infamous 1907 poem 'A Wine of Wizardry', and it was the young man's own gift for poetry that eventually brought him to the attention of the more experienced writer in 1911.

It was possibly with the help of his friend and mentor that Smith selected the contents of his first collection of verse, *The Star-Treader and Other Poems* (1912), published when the author was just eighteen years old. Issued by Sterling's own publisher, A.M. Robertson, in an estimated first edition of 2,000 copies, there is some conjecture that half the print run was destroyed in a fire. A photograph of the young poet was laid into a number of copies.

The slim volume was immediately hailed as the work of a prodigy and compared to the verse of Lord Byron, Christina

Rossetti and others. The newspapers acclaimed Smith as the "Boy Genius of the Sierras" and as the "Keats of the Pacific Coast", and the young poet's fame even spread across the Atlantic when, in a 1916 edition of the London *Evening News*, the Welsh fantasist Arthur Machen reviewed the book and observed that the author "shows in many of his verses a great admiration for 'the grand manner'; he builds his poems up as if they were cathedrals".

However, despite the almost overwhelmingly positive reaction of the critics, Smith later expressed his bitterness at receiving a total royalty of just $50.00 for sales totalling more than 1,400 copies by 1920.

Odes and Sonnets (1918) was Smith's next book. It was published on hand-made paper by the prestigious Book Club of California in a deluxe edition of only 300 copies, with a new introduction by Sterling.

As the market for poetry continued to decline, Smith was forced to self-publish *Ebony and Crystal: Poems in Verse and Prose* (1922) in a signed and numbered edition of 500 copies at $2.00 each. Along with a significant number of fantastic prose poems, this book also included the first publication of his epic verse, 'The Hashish-Eater; or, The Apocalypse of Evil'.

"Let him who is worthy by reason of his clear eye and unjaded heart wander across these borders of beauty and mystery and be glad," entreated Sterling in his preface to the book, while H.P. Lovecraft described Smith's poetry as evoking "realms of exalted and iridescent strangeness beyond space and time yet real as any reality because dreams have made them so".

It was this visionary quality of Smith's poetry and art that caught Lovecraft's attention, and while he was visiting his friend Samuel Loveman in Cleveland. Lovecraft sent Smith a letter on August 12, 1922, praising his drawings and watercolours: "What a world of opiate phantasy & horror is here unveiled, & what an unique power & perspective must lie behind it!". After describing his own writing, Lovecraft concluded, "I should deem it a great honour to hear from you if you have the leisure & inclination to address an obscurity".

Smith did reply, and he soon began corresponding regularly with, as Lovecraft described himself, "an obscure companion in the realms of the macabre". It was not long before Lovecraft was suggesting that Smith illustrate his stories for the small press magazines and gushing that "The magnificence of 'The Hashish-Eater' is beyond description".

Lovecraft, who would often use playful nicknames when writing to his many correspondents, soon began addressing Smith as "Klarkash-Ton" while often phonetically signing his own letters "E'ch-Pi-El".

At Lovecraft's urging, Smith also began corresponding with members of the so-called "Lovecraft Circle"—other writers such as Donald Wandrei, August W. Derleth and Frank Belknap Long, Jr.

"I doubt if any young writer today can fully understand what it meant to be in frequent correspondence with so inspired and volumi-nous a letter writer as H.P. Lovecraft," recalled Long many years later.

Wandrei and Smith quickly became friends, and when, in 1925, Smith needed another $50.00 before he could publish his fourth book of poetry, *Sandalwood*, Wandrei immediately sent him a cheque, despite only having $65.00 at the time. The volume appeared in a signed and numbered edition of 250 copies.

With George Sterling's assistance, Wandrei's early article about Smith, 'The Emperor of Dreams', appeared in the December 1926 issue of *The Overland Monthly*. However Sterling never lived to see it published, having apparently committed suicide by swallowing cyanide the month before. Smith's appreciation of his friend and adviser appeared the following March in the same West Coast magazine.

Weird Tales

JAN. 1932 — *The Unique Magazine* — 25 CENTS

The MONSTER OF THE PROPHECY
by Clark Ashton Smith

GASTON LEROUX
S. B. H. HURST
G. G. PENDARVES
FRANK B. LONG
AUGUST W. DERLETH
ALEXANDRE DUMAS

V

"It is my own theory that if the infinite worlds of the cosmos were opened to human vision, the visionary would be overwhelmed by horror in the end."

—Clark Ashton Smith

I T WAS THE American Depression, and despite having achieved significant acclaim, if only on a regional basis, Clark Ashton Smith received little financial reward for his poetry. He survived on odd jobs and a number of small stipends.

Lovecraft had recommended his Californian pen-pal to *Weird Tales* editor Edwin Baird and even sent him some sample verse, and two short poems ('The Red Moon' and 'The Garden of Evil') appeared in the July–August 1923 issue of the magazine. Although they were buried away in the back of the publication, and not even listed on the Contents page, Smith still managed to beat Lovecraft into the pulp by two issues.

In the summer of 1927, during a camping trip to the mountains, his close female acquaintance Genevieve K. Sully criticised Smith's lack of ambition and advised him to "do something with himself".

"His financial situation at that time was critical," she recalled in 1967, "and some practical advice seemed in order. This prodding led to Clark's writing of weird fiction."

Lovecraft also encouraged his friend to turn his visions of

cosmic horror and fantasy into prose and send the results to *Weird Tales*.

Inspired by the French Decadence movement of the late 19th century—perhaps best exemplified by "the father of modern poetry", Charles Pierre Baudelaire (who in turn was inspired by the works of Edgar Allan Poe)—Smith's characters were often led to their death or damnation by the lure of the exotic. It has been argued that Smith shared the *ennui* of the Decadents, yet he taught himself to read and write in Spanish and French just so that he could read and translate his favourite poets in those languages.

Although Clark Ashton Smith's stories had previously appeared in such publications as *The Overland Monthly*, *The Black Cat* and *10 Story Book*, it was not until 1928 that he began writing short fiction full-time. For scarcely the next decade, he turned out stories at the rate of one a month, despite detailed revisions which usually resulted in him producing around five drafts of each tale.

"Take one step across the threshold of his stories and you plunge into colour, sound, taste, smell and texture—into language," Ray Bradbury observed.

Smith later confided in a January 1931 letter to Lovecraft that his writing of weird fiction became "an imaginative escape from the human aquarium", but added that he was "finding a pleasure in fiction-writing, and deriving a mental 'kick' from it which I seldom got from poetry".

Smith had translated a number of Baudelaire's poems from the French for *Weird Tales*, and although he had been selling his own poetry to the title since 1923, with the publication of 'The Ninth Skeleton' in the September 1928 issue he began a twenty-five-year run in the magazine with just over sixty stories. Smith even illustrated some of his own early work in *Weird Tales*, for which Wright paid him $7.00 apiece.

"Speaking as a reader," wrote Smith in the December 1930 letters column 'The Eyrie', "I should like to say that *Weird Tales* is the one magazine that gives its writers ample imaginative freeway." Not surprisingly, given his own proclivity for such tales, in the April 1932 issue he suggested that "a representative number of *Weird Tales* should include a least one fantasy of poetic and atmospheric type".

The readership apparently agreed with him. In the April 1934 issue, Malcom Bethune from Berkeley, California, wrote: "Clark Ashton Smith's stories embody rare beauty and delicacy", while Joseph Hatch of Leavenworth, Kansas, praised the author in the same issue: "The way that fellow can paint imaginary scenes and make the reader see what he is talking about, is marvellous." In the June 1935 edition, Carroll F. Wales from Denmark, Maine, revealed: "I can't seem to get enough of Clark Ashton Smith. Usually when an author writes a story every month his work gets tiresome, but not Smith's".

Margaret St. Clair, who would later become a contributor herself, enthused in the June 1934 *Weird Tales*: "As long as WT prints stories by Clark Ashton Smith, however, I'll keep reading it. His tales have a rounded jewel-like self-containedness that is, artistically, a delight…And Smith's drawings are, I think, by far the best in the magazine." Future poet Emil Petaja concurred in the August 1935 issue: "Clark Ashton Smith remains as ever—the poet whose tales waft one into far-off enchanted lands".

However, there was the occasional minor caveat, such as that from Herbert V. Ross of London, England, in the June 1938 edition: "Smith is a true artist of words, and I hope we shall have many more of his stories, and translations of Baudelaire. Mr. Smith, you're a genius, you're number one, but why will you dwell on the horror instead of the exotic and beautiful?" Robert Burrell also complained from Corona, California, in the October 1938 edition: "I was somewhat disappointed with Clark Ashton Smith with his 'Mother of Toads', when he usually writes so charmingly of the people and forest of Averoigne".

Between 1928 and 1937, Smith produced more than 100 short stories, which he would often compose on the back of discarded typescripts of previous tales. Half of his fiction belonged to various story cycles set on dream-worlds and alien landscapes or in colourful and exotic imaginary lands with their own unique cultures, languages and mythologies.

"I am far happier when I can create *everything* in a story—including the milieu," Smith wrote to Lovecraft in 1930. "I haven't enough love for, or interest in, real places to invest them with the atmosphere that I achieve in something purely imaginative."

Amongst the fantastic locales Smith created were the prehistoric continent of Hyperborea; the super-civilisation of Atlantis, also known as Poseidonis; and the alien worlds of Xiccarph and Mars.

However, his most successful imaginary regions were Zothique—the last inhabited continent on Earth, where sorcery and demonism prevail again as in ancient days—and the vampire-haunted mediaeval province of Averoigne.

In a playful letter to Lovecraft in 1931, Smith revealed: "I have heard it hinted in certain obscure and arcanic prophecies that the far-future continent called Gnydron by some and Zothique by others, which will rise millions of years hence in what is now the South Atlantic...and will witness the intrusion of Things from galaxies not yet visible; and worse than this, a hideously chaotic breaking-down of dimensional barriers which will leave parts of our world in other dimensions, and vice versa."

Smith's story-cycle about the dying continent of Zothique began with 'The Empire of the Necromancers' in the September 1932 *Weird Tales*. The author observed that the story's "queer mood" was "much over-greened with what H.P. [Lovecraft] once referred to as the 'verdigris of decadence'".

However, *Weird Tales* initially rejected the first version of another story, 'The Beast of Averoigne'. In a letter dated July 10,

1932, Smith confided to August Derleth that "the documentary mode of presentation may have led me into more archaism than was palatable". Derleth suggested some changes to the story, which led Smith to cut it by 1,400 words, and the revised version appeared in the May 1933 issue of the pulp. Smith admitted: "I think that I have done better tales, but few that are technically superior".

Lovecraft famously claimed that his friend had "one of the most opulent and fastidiously choice vocabularies ever commanded by a writer of English".

With a poet's grasp of language and tone, Smith had command of a comprehensive vocabulary which he obtained as a child by studying and learning an unabridged dictionary from A to Z and then each word's derivations from other languages.

In a 1930 letter to Lovecraft, Smith likened his own prose to "a verbal black magic, in the achievement of which I make use of prose-rhythm, metaphor, simile, tone-colour, counterpoint, and other stylistic resources, like a sort of incantation".

Writing to S.J. Sackett in 1950, he reiterated: "As to my employment of an ornate style, using many words of classic origin and exotic colour, I can only say that it is designed to produce effects of language and rhythm which could not possibly be achieved by a vocabulary restricted to what is known as 'basic English'".

Smith had also said much the same thing in a 1937 letter to *Weird Tales* artist Virgil Finlay: "I doubt if any of my work will ever have a wide public appeal, since the ideation and esthetics [sic] of my tales and poems are too remote from the psychology of the average reader. It is reassuring, however, that my work should appeal so strongly to a few."

Smith's first cover on *Weird Tales* was for 'The Monster of the Prophecy' (January, 1932). It was one of the author's "favourite yarns", although he was willing to bet "that the satiric implications will be missed by a lot of readers". Curtis C. Senf's outlandish illustration depicted a three-eyed alien creature menacing a cowering woman. Smith was quite proud of the story, which he completed in December 1929.

Unfortunately, a proposed sequel the following year entitled 'Vizaphmal in Ophiuchus', which would "not bring in any human beings at all", was planned but never written.

Along with such titles as *Weird Tales*, *Strange Tales*, *Oriental Stories* and *The Magic Carpet Magazine*, Smith also became a prolific contrib-utor of "super-scientific tales" to such pulps as *Wonder Stories*, *Astounding Stories*, *Comet Stories*, *Amazing Stories*, *Amazing Detective Tales*, *Thrilling Wonder Stories*, *Startling Stories* and *Stirring Science Stories*.

"Among those of my stories that can be classed, more or less accurately, as science fiction," explained Smith in 1940, "the majority have dealt either with worlds remote in space, or worlds hidden from human perception by their different vibratory rate or atomic composition."

He also revealed in his 1950 letter to S.J. Sackett: "It is my own theory that if the infinite worlds of the cosmos were opened to human vision, the visionary would be overwhelmed by horror in the end."

Smith's next "book", *The Immortals of Mercury*, appeared in wraps from Hugo Gernsback's Stellar Publishing Corporation in 1932 as "Science Fiction Series #16". With a cover price of ten cents, it was the author's first separately published fiction. However, he dismissed it as "A lot of tripe" and went on to observe, "but if it brings me a 200.00 dollar check, will have served its purpose".

As well as the genre magazines, Smith's poetry and fiction were also featured in *The Yale Review*, *The London Mercury*, *Munsey's*, *Asia*, *Wings*, *Poetry: A Magazine of Verse*, *The Philippine Magazine* and the *Mencken Smart Set*. His poetry was collected in numerous anthologies, and his translations of Baudelaire's *Les Fleurs du Mal* were included in *Flowers of Evil*, published for Members of the

Limited Editions Club by the Fanfare Press of London in 1940 in a limited edition of 1,500 copies.

In 1933, Smith began corresponding with another member of the Lovecraft and *Weird Tales* circle, Robert E. Howard. In a letter written during the summer of that year, the Texas author complimented his West Coast colleague: "How I envy your superb gift of conjuring up images of wizardry and wonder, like clouds rising from the ocean".

Little did they know that their correspondence would last barely three years.

VI

"Every now and then one of us finds the going
too hard and blows his brains out, but it's all
in the game, I reckon."

—Robert E. Howard

R OBERT ERVIN HOWARD was born in the fading ex-
cowtown of Peaster, Texas, about forty-five miles west of
Fort Worth, on January 22, 1906. He was the only son of Dr. Isaac
Mordecai Howard and Hester Jane (Ervin) Howard. The couple
met while living in Mineral Wells, in Palo Pinto County, and were
married on January 24, 1904.

Named after his great-grandfather, Robert Ervin, Howard later
revealed in a 1931 biographical sketch: "I come of old pioneer
American stock. By nationality I am predominantly Gaelic, in spite
of my English name—some three-fourths Irish, while the rest is a
mixture of English, Highland Scotch [sic], and Danish...
Practically all my life has been spent in the country and small
towns, outside of a few brief sojourns in New Orleans and some of
the Texas cities."

After moving around the state and living briefly in a number
of different locales, in September 1919 the family finally settled in
the small oil boom town of Cross Plains, in Callahan County,
Texas. Howard would live there for the rest of his life.

"As my father had his practise and did not attempt to run a farm, I had more leisure time than the average country kid," Howard later recalled. "I lived pretty much the average life of the time and place. Then (as now) I had more enemies than friends, but I did not lack companionship of my own age. I played the rough and savage games popular in those parts then, wrestled, hunted a little, fished a little, trapped a little, stole watermelons, went swimming, and spent more time than all in wandering about over the countryside on foot or on horseback."

Suffering from poor health (probably rheumatic fever) as a child—something he had in common with H.P. Lovecraft and Clark Ashton Smith—he once told his father, "Dad, when I was in school, I had to take a lot because I was alone and no one to take my part, so I intend to build my body until when anyone crosses me up, I can with my bare hands tear him to pieces, double him up, and break his back with my hands alone."

Although he started attending school when he was eight, Howard was mostly self-educated and read voraciously, revealing in one letter: "In my passionate quest for reading material, nothing could have halted me but a bullet through the head."

Despite hating "the clock-like regularity" of school, in 1923 he graduated at the age of seventeen from Brownwood High School and, not being able to afford college, attended the Commercial School at Howard Payne College in Brownwood, where he studied non-credit courses in shorthand, typing, book-keeping and commercial law.

In her 1986 memoir about Howard, *One Who Walked Alone*, former Cross Plains high school teacher Novalyne Price Ellis described her first meeting with the author in the late spring of 1933: "He was not dressed as I thought a writer should dress. His cap was pulled down low on his forehead. He had on a dingy white shirt and some loose-fitting brown pants that only came to his ankles and the top of his high-buttoned shoes. He took off his cap and I saw that his hair was dark brown, short, almost clipped. He ran his hand over his head."

E. Hoffman Price was one of the few writers and fellow correspondents who actually visited Howard. In 1934 he drove down to Cross Plains and recalled years later meeting a "... broad, towering man with a bluff, tanned face and a big, hearty hand, and a voice which was surprisingly soft and easy, instead of the bull-bellow one would expect of the creator of Conan and those other swashbucklers... Robert Howard was packed with whimsy and poetry which rang out in his letters, and blazed up in much of his published fiction but, as is usually the case with writers, his appearance belied him. His face was boyish, not yet having squared off into angles; his blue eyes, slightly prominent, had a wide-openness which did not suggest anything of the man's keen wit and agile fancy. That first picture persists—a powerful, solid, round faced fellow, kindly and somewhat stolid."

However, Price also discovered that there was a darker side to Howard while his host was driving Price and his new wife, Wanda, to the nearby town of Brownwood for a shopping and sight-seeing trip: "Suddenly, he took his foot off the throttle, cocked his head, idled down. We were approaching a clump of vegetation which was near the roadside. He reached across us, and to the side pocket. He took out a pistol, sized up the terrain, put the weapon back again, and resumed speed. He explained, in a matter-of-fact tone, 'I have a lot of enemies, everyone has around here. Wasn't that I figured we were running into anything but I had to make sure.'"

Some time later Howard confided to Novalyne Price Ellis that a man with as many enemies as he had needed to be careful. "Anybody who is not your friend is your enemy," he explained pleasantly to her.

Howard recalled that the first story he ever wrote, around the age of nine or ten, "Dealt with the adventures of one Boealf, a young Dane Viking" who he turned "loose on the Saxons with gusto".

"I took up writing simply because it seemed to promise an easier mode of work, more money, and more freedom than any job I'd tried," he explained later. "I wouldn't write otherwise."

At the age of fifteen he wrote his first professional story, 'Bill Smally and the Power of the Human Eye', and sent it off to the pulp magazine *Adventure*. It was rejected, and the author always blamed his inability to ever sell to one of his favourite periodicals on this initial failure, and it was another three years before Howard made his professional debut in the pulp magazine *Weird Tales*.

Around this same time, he created two characters that he would return to later in his career—two-fisted adventurer Steve Allison (who he would reinvent as a Western gunslinger) and Francis X. Gordon, whose Oriental exploits were undoubtedly inspired by the type of fiction he was reading in *Adventure*.

"I'm narrow in my literary likings," admitted Howard. "About the only poets and writers I can stand are the British and American ones. English poetry is probably the highest form of English literature. My favourite writers are A. Conan Doyle, Jack London, Mark Twain, Sax Rohmer, Jeffery Farnol, Talbot Mundy, Harold Lamb, R.W. Chambers, Rider Haggard, Kipling, Sir Walter Scott, Lane-Poole, Jim Tully, Ambrose Bierce, Arthur Machen, Edgar Allan Poe, and H.P. Lovecraft."

From the summer of 1930 onwards, Howard and Lovecraft conducted a lively correspondence. It fell to the Rhode Island writer to pen Howard's obituary in the September 1936 issue of Julius Schwartz's *Fantasy Magazine*, where he explained: "Not only did he excel in pictures of strife and slaughter, but he was almost alone in his ability to create real emotions of spectral fear and dread suspense. No author—even in the humblest fields—can truly excel unless he takes his work very seriously; and Mr. Howard did just that even in cases where he consciously thought he did not."

Although many of his early stories never sold or were never completed, Howard persevered with his ambition to be a writer. At the age of eighteen, while taking courses in shorthand and typing at Howard Payne College in Brownwood, he made his first professional sale to *Weird Tales*.

At the time Howard began submitting manuscripts, Farnsworth Wright had replaced Edwin F. Baird as editor of the Chicago-based magazine, after founder and owner J.C. Henneberger was forced to reorganise the business owing to debts. From the November 1924 issue onwards, *Weird Tales* began to flourish under Wright's guidance.

In fact, Wright initially accepted three stories from the fledgling Texas writer, and Robert E. Howard made his debut in the pages of "The Unique Magazine" with the caveman adventure 'Spear and Fang'.

Published in the July 1925 issue, its teenage author was paid the princely sum of $16.00 at half-a-cent a word upon publication. Even in pre-Depression Texas that would not go far, and Howard quickly realised that he would have to work at a variety of jobs to supplement his meagre income from writing. These included picking cotton, branding cattle, hauling garbage, working in a grocery store and a law office, jerking soda in a drug store, trying to be a public stenographer, packing a surveyor's rod and working up oil field news for some Texas and Oklahoma papers. However, by his own admission, he "... wasn't a success at any of them".

In his 1931 biographical sketch he told Wright: "Pounding out a living at the writing game is no snap—but the average man's life is no snap, whatever he does. I'm merely one of a huge army, all of whom are bucking the line one way or another for meat for their bellies—which is the main basic principle and reason and eventual goal of Life. Every now and then one of us finds the going too hard and blows his brains out, but it's all in the game, I reckon."

These were to be tragically prophetic words.

Thanks to Wright and *Weird Tales*, things soon began to change for Howard. In just three years his income from writing jumped from $772.50 to $1,500.26. The prolific author also began to sell other types of fiction—Westerns, sports stories, horror tales, true confessions, historical adventures and detective thrillers—to pulp markets besides *Weird Tales*, such as *Argosy All-Story Weekly*, *Fight Stories* and *Ghost Stories*.

At the same time he began to develop a series of characters with whom he would forever be identified: the English Puritan swordsman Solomon Kane (actually created while he was still in high school); the king of fabled Valusia, King Kull; Pictish chieftain Bran Mak Morn; prize-fighter Sailor Steve Costigan; Celtic warrior Turlogh O'Brien; soldier of fortune Francis X. Gordon, also known as "El Borak"; humorous hillbilly Breckenridge Elkins, and of course the mighty barbarian, Conan the Cimmerian.

Like Lovecraft, many of Robert E. Howard's stories were based on dreams he had, as he revealed: "I am never, in these dreams of ancient times, a civilised man. Always I am the barbarian, the skin-clad, tousle-haired, light-eyed wild man, armed with a rude axe or sword, fighting the elements and wild beasts, or grappling with armoured hosts marching with the tread of civilised discipline from fallow fruitful lands and walled cities. This is reflected in my writings, too, for when I begin a tale of old times, I always find myself instinctively arrayed on the side of the barbarian, against the powers of organised civilisation."

The first of the author's memorable sword-wielding heroes—the grim Puritan adventurer Solomon Kane—made his first appearance in *Weird Tales* with the publication of 'Red Shadows' in the August 1928 issue, although the story had originally been simply titled after its protagonist when originally turned down by *Argosy All-Story Weekly* the previous year.

Howard had received a personal note from an associate editor at the magazine who told him, "You seem to have caught the knack of writing good action and plenty of it into your story".

Buoyed by this rejection, he sent the story off to *Weird Tales*, who published it without any major changes.

As H.P. Lovecraft later recalled: "In August, 1928, began the tales dealing with Solomon Kane, an English Puritan of relentless duelling and wrong-redressing practices whose adventures took him to strange and primordial cities in the African jungle. With these tales Mr. Howard struck what proved to be one of his most effective accomplishments—the description of vast megalithic cities of the elder world, around whose dark towers and labyrinthine nether vaults linger an aura of pre-human fear and necromancy which no other writer could duplicate. These tales also marked Mr. Howard's development of that skill and zest in depicting sanguinary conflict which became so typical his work. Solomon Kane, like several other heroes of the author was conceived in boyhood long before incorporation in any story."

Armed with a rapier and a brace of flintlock pistols, along with the mystical Staff of Solomon given to him by his friend N'Longa, the sombre adventurer took his battle against evil across Europe and into the darkest jungles of Africa.

"Solomon Kane I created when I was in high school, at the age of about sixteen," recalled Howard. "Several years passed before I put him on paper. He was probably the result of an admiration for a certain type of cold, steely-nerved duellist that existed in the 16th century".

In his first published story, Kane pursued a villain known as Le Loup from France to Africa to avenge the death of a young girl. He also first encountered the ancient native shaman, N'Longa. Farnsworth Wright was impressed enough to give 'Red Shadows' pride of place on the cover of *Weird Tales*, with an illustration by artist Curtis C. Senf.

Five months later saw the publication of 'Skulls in the Stars' in the same magazine. For this tale, Kane's route took him across a haunted English moor. With 'Rattle of Bones' in the June 1929 *Weird Tales*, Kane found himself sharing a German inn with the remains of a sorcerer.

Published over the June and July 1930 issues, 'The Moon of Skulls' returned Kane to Africa, where he travelled to the lost city of Negari and encountered its vampire queen. Hugh Rankin supplied the stylish cover illustration for the first part, while the second instalment was voted the most popular story in that issue of *Weird Tales* by the readers.

The following month, Kane was still in Africa for 'The Hills of the Dead', in which he first received the supernatural staff from N'Longa and encountered the walking dead.

"Robert E. Howard's Solomon Kane stories have me pleading for more stories about the adventures of this likeable character," requested a contributor to the letters column, 'The Eyrie'. "Please induce Mr. Howard to give us a sequel—and still more sequels— about this Kane person."

However, despite this kind of enthusiasm for the character, it was more than a year before 'The Footfalls Within' appeared in the September 1931 *Weird Tales*. This time Kane became involved with Arab slave-traders.

The final Solomon Kane story to be published in the magazine was 'Wings in the Night', which appeared in the July 1932 issue. Again set in Africa, the gloomy Puritan investigated a village destroyed by a race of flying creatures that spawned the legend of the Harpies.

Of course, Howard had barely ever travelled outside his native state of Texas, but he used what he had read in books to give verisimilitude to the foreign locales in his stories.

Following Howard's premature death, the poem 'Solomon Kane's Homecoming' was published in 1936 in the first and only edition of Wilson Shepherd and Donald A. Wollheim's fanzine *Fanciful Tales of Time and Space*.

"I know nothing about the mechanics of poetry," admitted Howard. "I write the stuff by ear, so to speak, and my musical ear is very full of flaws. I never devoted over thirty minutes to any rhyme in my life, though I've spent hours memorising the poetry of other men."

Lovecraft was more complimentary about his verse: "Mr. Howard's poetry—weird, warlike, and adventurous—was no less notable than his prose. It had the true spirit of the ballad and the epic, and was marked by a pulsing rhythm and potent imagery of the extreme distinctive cast."

THE MIRRORS of TUZUN THUNE

ROBERT E. HOWARD

"Kull!" The yell split the silence into
a million vibratory fragments.

"A wild, weird clime that lieth sublime
Out of Space, out of Time."

—Poe.

THERE comes, even to kings,
the time of great weariness.
Then the gold of the throne
is brass, the silk of the palace be-
comes drab. The gems in the diadem
and upon the fingers of the women
sparkle drearily like the ice of the
white seas; the speech of men is as
the empty rattle of a jester's bell
and the feel comes of things unreal;
even the sun is copper in the sky
and the breath of the green ocean is
no longer fresh.

Kull sat upon the throne of Valusia and the hour of weariness was
upon him. They moved before him
in an endless, meaningless pano-
rama, men, women, priests, events
and shadows of events; things seen
and things to be attained. But like
shadows they came and went, leaving no trace upon his consciousness,
save that of a great mental fatigue.
Yet Kull was not tired. There was
a longing in him for things beyond
himself and beyond the Valusian
court. An unrest stirred in him and
strange, luminous dreams roamed
his soul. At his bidding there came
to him Brule the Spear-slayer, warrior of Pictland, from the islands
beyond the West.

"Lord king, you are tired of the
life of the court. Come with me upon
my galley and let us roam the tides
for a space."

"Nay." Kull rested his chin

VII

"Of these the central figure was King Kull of Valusia."
—H.P. Lovecraft

EXACTLY A YEAR after the Solomon Kane story 'Red Shadows' appeared in *Weird Tales* in 1928, Howard introduced readers to another new hero: Kull was king of Valusia, and his adventures were set in a distant Pre-Cataclysmic Age that predated the destruction of Atlantis and Lemuria.

"About Atlantis," Howard wrote to his friend Harold Preece in October 1928, "I believe something of the sort existed, though I do not especially hold any theory about a high type of civilisation existing there—in fact, I doubt that. But some continent was submerged away back, or some large body of land, for practically all peoples have legends about a flood."

In the same letter, the author went on tell Preece that he had included a long letter to Farnsworth Wright which he expected to be published as a foreword to his story 'The Shadow Kingdom', which he had sold to *Weird Tales* for $100.

Unfortunately, when the story finally appeared, it was without an introduction and the letter to the editor apparently no longer survives.

In the story, former warrior and mercenary Kull had recently become king of Valusia, and his power over the kingdom was already being threatened by a pre-human race of Serpent Men.

"This tale I wove about a mythical antediluvian empire," revealed Howard, "a contemporary of Atlantis."

Considered by some to be the first American "heroic fantasy" or "sword-and-sorcery" story, 'The Shadow Kingdom' formed the foundation—literally—of Howard's later development of Conan. So much so that, in his 1932 essay 'The Hyborian Age', the author went to great pains to link his two mythologies with a common history.

As H.P. Lovecraft observed: "Always a keen student of Celtic antiquities and other phases of remote history, Mr. Howard began in 1929—with 'The Shadow Kingdom', in the August *Weird Tales*— that succession of tales of the prehistoric world for which he soon grew so famous. The earlier specimens described a very distant age in man's history—when Atlantis, Lemuria and Mu were above the waves, and when the shadows of pre-human reptile men rested upon the primal scene. Of these the central figure was King Kull of Valusia."

'The Shadow Kingdom' was voted the best story in the issue by the readers of *Weird Tales*.

Between 1926 and 1929, the author wrote thirteen stories and a poem featuring Kull. Three of these tales remained unfinished.

Of the completed stories, only 'The Shadow Kingdom', 'The Mirrors of Tuzun Thune' and 'Kings of the Night' (in which Kull played a supporting role) were published during the author's lifetime.

At least three other Kull stories were submitted to *Weird Tales* and rejected by Farnsworth Wright, while another two failed to sell to *Argosy*.

It was therefore no surprise that when Lovecraft suggested in 1934 that he write more stories about Kull, Howard responded: "Thanks for the kind things you said about the Kull stories, but I doubt if I'll ever be able to write another. The three stories I wrote about that character seemed almost to write themselves, without any planning on my part; there was no conscious effort on my part to work them up. They simply grew up, unsummoned, full grown in my mind and flowed out on paper from my finger tips. To sit down and consciously try to write another story on that order would be to produce something the artificiality of which would be apparent."

As Howard had revealed the year before in a letter to Clark Ashton Smith: "Suddenly I would find myself out of contact with the conception, as if the man himself had been standing at my shoulder directing my efforts, and had suddenly turned and gone away, leaving me to search for another character".

Despite regular requests from readers for more adventures about Kull, no other stories featuring the character appeared in *Weird Tales* after 1930. However, the poem 'The King and the Oak' eventually saw posthumous publication in the February 1939 issue.

THE HAUNTED CHAIR *by* Gaston Leroux *The* PHANTOM *of the* OPERA AUTHOR OF THE

Weird Tales

The Unique Magazine

DEC.
1931

25¢
30c IN CANADA

The DARK MAN

by Robert E. Howard

Otis
Adelbert
Kline

Edmond
Hamilton

Alexandre
Dumas

VIII

"To me 'Pict' must always refer to the small dark
Mediterranean aborigines of Britain."
—Robert E. Howard

KULL'S CHIEF ALLY was Brule the Spear-slayer, a Pictish
warrior, even though the Atlanteans were hereditary
enemies of all Picts. Since his earliest attempts to become a writer,
Robert E. Howard had always been fascinated by the history of the
Picts, and they had featured in a number of his tales over the years.

As he revealed in a 1932 letter to H.P. Lovecraft: "There is one
hobby of mine which puzzles me to this day. That is my interest in
the people which, for the sake of brevity, I have always designated
as Picts...to me 'Pict' must always refer to the small dark
Mediterranean aborigines of Britain".

The second story from Howard accepted by *Weird Tales* was
'The Lost Race', a historical tale about the Picts, who were depicted
as the savage remnant of a pre-Celtic civilisation that had been
driven underground. It finally appeared two years later in the
January 1927 issue, after editor Farnsworth Wright had sent it back
for revisions. Howard was paid $37.50.

However, when the author submitted 'Men of the Shadows' to
the magazine in 1926, it was rejected by Wright for having "too
little of a 'story', despite the vigorous action in the opening pages".

Although the editor suggested another market that might take it after revisions, the story remained unpublished until the late 1960s.

The tale also introduced the last pure-blood Pictish chieftain, Bran Mak Morn—a descendent of Brule the Spear-Slayer—and his struggle against the invading Roman forces. The character had been another of those that the young Howard had created early in his career—including an unfinished play, written when the author was around sixteen or seventeen years old—but which he had been unable to do anything with.

Howard's next attempts to sell stories about Bran Mak Morn and the Picts to *Weird Tales* were more successful. 'Kings of the Night' and 'The Dark Man' were both submitted to the magazine in March 1930. The former tale, which featured both Bran Mak Morn and Kull united through sorcery, appeared in the November issue that year.

"Red battle raged when Kull, king of Valusia, came from out of the mists of his Shadow Kingdom to lead the Norsemen in a fierce fight against the Roman Legionnaires" trumpeted the October issue's preview.

It proved to be the most popular story published in *Weird Tales* for the entire year.

Meanwhile, 'The Dark Man'—featuring outcast Irish outlaw Turlogh Dubh O'Brien, and in which a magical statue of Bran Mak Morn played an important role—was published in the December 1931 *Weird Tales*. C.C. Senf was again chosen to depict Howard's story on the cover of the magazine.

However, not everyone was impressed with the tale. When a reader complained that it was not "weird" enough, another contributor to 'The Eyrie' came to the author's defence in the April 1932 issue: "In all courtesy," politely wrote Kirk Mashburn from Houston, Texas, "I disagree with Mr. Paul S. Smith's criticism, printed in The Eyrie of the February issue, of Robert E. Howard's yarn, 'The Dark Man'. The entire plot of this story, and a considerable part of the action—the *adventure*—pivots on the active intervention of the Dark Man himself. By implications so strong as to leave the reader no alternate solution, the author justifies the Picts in believing the spirit of their ancient king to inhabit the image *and give it personality*. In other words, for the purpose of the story, the belief is fact. This is certainly a fantastic note, to put it mildly. I believe your readers, in the main, agree with me in liking Mr. Howard's stories not only for their own sake, when they run in the vein of 'The Dark Man', but because they make an admirable and harmonious foil to frankly supernatural or horror stories. I would like it understood that I express my personal liking for the story, without in any sense attempting or wishing to deny Mr. Smith's rights to his own preferences."

The story was reprinted in the final issue of the original run of *Weird Tales*, in September 1954.

As Howard revealed in a biographical letter to Alvin Earl Perry, published in *Fantasy Magazine* in July 1935: "The first character I ever created was Francis X. Gordon, El Borak, the hero of 'The Daughter of Erlik Khan' (*Top-Notch*), etc. I don't remember his genesis. He came to life in my mind when I was about ten years old. The next was Bran Mak Morn, the Pictish king ('The Kings of the Night', etc. *Weird Tales*). He was the result of my discovery of the existence of the Pictish race, when reading some historical works in a public library in New Orleans at the age of thirteen. Physically he bore a striking resemblance to El Borak."

Howard was paid $120 for 'Kings of the Night' and, in a letter to writer Tevis Clyde Smith in September 1930, the author disclosed: "Some ways this story is the best I ever wrote. Nothing very weird about it, but good battle stuff, if I do say so myself."

In fact, Howard's final tale of Bran Mak Morn actually turned out to be his best. Described by editor Wright as "an unusually fine story", 'Worms of the Earth' was published in the November 1932 *Weird Tales*. The author admitted in a letter to H.P. Lovecraft that he "must have been unusually careless" when he wrote the story, given the number of errors it contained.

"Mr. Howard had written many tales of the early Picts and Celts," Lovecraft noted later, "including a notable series revolving round the chieftain Bran Mak Morn. Few readers will ever forget the hideous and compelling power of that macabre masterpiece, 'Worms of the Earth.'"

"His best story is perhaps 'Worms of the Earth,'" agreed August Derleth, as did this anonymous contributor to 'The Eyrie':

"Robert E. Howard's 'Worms of the Earth' is a story that has *everything*—vividly drawn characters—intense, sustained, powerful atmosphere—it is utterly different from anybody else's stories—perfect illusion from first sentence to last—and he even manages to inject admiration for a character into a weird story. I definitely admire this man's passionate feeling that his subjects are his children and he's honour bound to be loyal to them. This story is a perfect thing. It's like a champion dog in an all-breeds event. I can stack it up against stories of a wholly different breed and it still holds its own."

In this superior novella, Bran entered into an unwholesome pact with a monstrous race of subterranean creatures to take revenge on a brutal Roman governor. This race of underground dwellers—also referred to as "the Little People" or "the Children of the Night"— was a theme that the author had worked with before in a couple of other stories. At the time, Howard was apparently influenced by the work of Welsh author Arthur Machen and various ideas suggested by his friend Lovecraft.

The story was reprinted in the October 1939 *Weird Tales*.

Howard acknowledged in a letter to Lovecraft that, when he came to write about the Picts, it was through the eyes of other characters. "Only in my last Bran story, 'The Worms of the Earth' which Mr. Wright accepted, did I look through Pictish eyes, and speak with a Pictish tongue!"

In a memoir published in 1968, writer Harold Preece recounted an evening in December in 1928, when he and Howard went out into the surrounding Texas countryside to get drunk and talk. Amongst the topics they discussed were the fairies and leprechauns of Celtic legend.

"The Little People, he said, were remnants of Europe's original inhabitants," Preece recalled, "forced to retreat into caves and other subterranean hideaways after the advent of those tall conquerors who would come to be known as the Indo-Europeans. From his account, the small, dark aborigines ventured forth only by night to stretch their limbs dancing, and to forage by shooting their neighbour's cattle with stone-tipped arrows. Superstitious peasants would chance upon the fairy gatherings at night and imagine them to be convocations of supernatural beings, hence all the feyish mythology found throughout rural Europe, particularly in the Celtic countries."

The year after it first appeared in *Weird Tales*, 'Worms of the Earth' marked Howard's first British hardcover publication when editor Christine Campbell Thomson selected it for her volume *Keep on the Light*, the ninth in the popular "Not at Night" anthology series from publisher Selwyn & Blount.

Fascinating Tales of the East

ALL STORIES COMPLETE

ORIENTAL STORIES

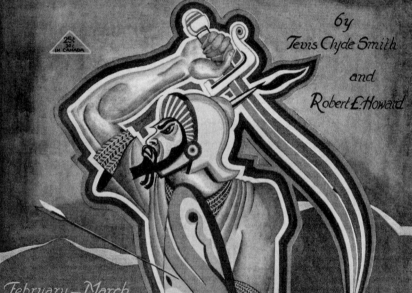

RED BLADES OF BLACK CATHAY

by
Tevis Clyde Smith
and
Robert E. Howard

25¢
30¢
IN CANADA

February — March
1931

IX

"There is no literary work, to me, half as zestful as
rewriting history in the guise of fiction."

—Robert E. Howard

I N 1930, THE owners of *Weird Tales*, Popular Fiction
Publishing Company, launched an adventure magazine entitled
Oriental Stories, also edited by Farnsworth Wright.

"All the Glamour, and Mystery of the Orient," promised the
hyperbolic advertisements for the first issue. "The Orient, land of
intrigues, red war and languorous loves, home of Harun al Raschid
the Just, Tamerlane the Magnificent, and Ghengis Khan the Red
Scourge. All the glitter and pageantry of Samarkand in the Valley
of of Zarab Shan, Herat of the Hundred Gardens, Bagdad,
Damascus, and the fabled cities of Cathay. Xanadu, home of Kubla
Khan; Bokhara, Mandalay, Singapore—the very names breathe
romance, adventure, and the mystery of hidden things. Devil-
dancing lamas of the inscrutable Tibet, the veiled allure of Oriental
harems, the charge of fierce Arab tribesmen, the dancing of
almond-eyed maidens under a Burmese moon, the barbaric
splendour of mediæval sultans, the ageless life of Egypt, and the
deathless allure of the *Thousand and One Nights*."

Not only were the readers unable to ignore this exotic
travelogue, but Robert E. Howard could not disregard Wright's

invitation to contribute to his new companion magazine. With his fascination for ancient history, Howard was soon a regular contributor with several tales about the Middle East and the Crusades, including 'Hawks of Outremer' and 'The Sowers of the Thunder'.

Although H.P. Lovecraft claimed, "His novelettes of oriental warfare displayed to the utmost his mastery of romantic swash-buckling," Howard had no pretensions that he was writing for posterity.

"One problem in writing bloody literature is to present it in such a manner as to avoid a suggestion of cheap blood-and-thunder melodrama," mused the author, "which is what some people will always call action, regardless of how realistic and true it is . . . Another problem is how far you can go without shocking the readers into distaste for your stuff—and therefore cutting down sales. I've always held myself down in writing action stories; I never let my stories be as bloody and brutal as the ages and the incidents I was trying to depict actually were."

E. Hoffman Price, who was the only *Weird Tales* writer to meet Howard, in 1934 and 1935, remembered that during one of these visits he bluntly told his friend: "Bob, the curtain line dialogue of 'The Sowers of the Thunder' are sheer bombast. They match the uttermost impossibility and incredibility of the entire yarn! It is pure manure! I wonder if you'd believe me when I tell you how many times I have re-read that yarn, and savoured that impossible-hokum dialogue!"

"Sure it was pure crap," replied Howard with a chuckle. "But sometimes you've got to do it that way."

Perhaps due to this adherence to commercialism, the author continued to complain about the lack of magazines that he could sell his work to: "I could never make a living writing such things, though; the markets are too scanty, with requirements too narrow, and it takes me so long to complete one. I try to write as true to the actual facts as possible; at least I try to commit as few errors as possible. I like to have my background and setting as accurate and realistic as I can, with my limited knowledge."

Unfortunately, *Oriental Stories* only lasted for nine issues. Sales were disappointing and, as a result, author payments were often months overdue. Following the publication of 'Lord of Samarcand' (originally written under the title 'The Lame Man') in the Spring 1932 issue, the title was re-launched in January 1933 as *The Magic Carpet Magazine*.

"Throughout space to the most distant corners of the universe in the twinkling of an eye!" announced the advertisements. "When Schehera-zade told her Sultan the tales that make up *The Arabian Nights Entertainments*, she told him of a Magic Carpet that flew through the sky and carried its human cargo to distant countries with the speed of thought.

"*The Magic Carpet Magazine*, like the carpet of Scheherazade, carries its readers out of the humdrum life of our modern civilisation to lands of romance, adventure, mystery and glamour."

Howard had three stories published in the retitled pulp—'The Lion of Tiberias', 'The Shadow of the Vulture', and another under his regular pseudonym "Patrick Ervin", 'Alleys of Darkness'. These latter two appeared in the January 1934 edition, which turned out to be the fifth and final issue.

At the time of the title's demise, several sports stories and two of the author's historical adventures remained in the magazine's inventory. One of the latter was a 14,000-word novella entitled 'The Road of the Eagles', which was later rewritten as a Conan story by L. Sprague de Camp.

"There is no literary work, to me, half as zestful as rewriting history in the guise of fiction," revealed Howard. "I wish I was able to devote the rest of my life to that kind of work. I could write a hundred years and still there would be stories clamouring to be written, by the scores. Every page of history teems with dramas that should be put on paper. A single paragraph may be packed with action and drama enough to fill a whole volume of fiction work."

However, not everyone agreed that these tales were amongst the author's best work. "It was clear that Bob's 'Oriental stuff' was conspicuously derivative," complained E. Hoffman Price. "In some areas, it was well researched. In others, an experienced writer would recognise at once the collection of clichés which he would have avoided—the substitutes for genuine, all-out verisimilitude."

Editor Farnsworth Wright had already mounted his own defence of the author's work in June 1935 when he wrote in 'The Eyrie': "Writers of historical fiction often take liberties with historical facts; just as Robert E. Howard took liberties with the facts about Tamerlane's death in one of his greatest stories, 'Lord of Samarcand'. But Mr. Howard, in spite of a version of Tamerlane's death which ran counter to the known facts, was true to the historic picture."

Around the same time as the creation of *Oriental Stories*, Popular Fiction had also planned to launch a second companion magazine, entitled *Strange Stories*. Although Howard had submitted 'Kings of the Night' to the proposed new market, Farnsworth Wright accepted it for *Weird Tales*.

However the author did sell both 'The Gods of Bal-Sagoth' and 'The Dark Man', featuring 11th Century Irishman Turlogh O'Brien, to the new title. Unfortunately, a dispute with Macfadden Publications—who had issued eight editions of a periodical entitled *True Strange Stories* in 1929—prevented the magazine from appearing, and Wright eventually published them in the October and December 1931 issues of *Weird Tales*, respectively. In fact, 'The Gods of Bal-Sagoth' was intended to be a sequel to 'The Dark Man', even though it appeared first.

Howard wrote all three of these tales intended for *Strange Stories* during an unusually productive period between February and March 1930.

JUNE—25¢

Weird Tales

BLACK COLOSSUS

BY

ROBERT E. HOWARD

HUGH B. CAVE—CLARK ASHTON SMITH—PAUL ERNST

X

"There are many things concerning Conan's life
of which I am not certain myself."

—Robert E. Howard

I N 1932, Robert E. Howard launched his most memorable character, Conan the Cimmerian, with 'The Phoenix on the Sword' in the December *Weird Tales*.

Conan soon became so popular in *Weird Tales* that Howard stopped writing about any other series characters for the magazine. However, with markets drying up around him, the author continued to churn out numerous other tales for any magazine that would take them.

At the same time he had sent Farnsworth Wright 'The Phoenix on the Sword'—and which the editor asked him to rewrite— Howard also submitted another Conan story entitled 'The Frost-Giant's Daughter'. Both these tales were revisions of unsold stories—'The Phoenix on the Sword' was a rewrite of the unsold King Kull tale 'By This Axe I Rule!' and 'The Frost-Giant's Daughter' was originally entitled 'The Frost King's Daughter'.

In a letter dated March 10, 1932, Wright responded: "I am returning 'The Frost-Giant's Daughter' in a separate envelope, as I do not much care for it."

Never much good at taking rejection, when Wright turned

down 'The Frost-Giant's Daughter'—apparently because it was a little too risqué for his tastes—Howard simply put the manuscript away and forgot about it.

However, in November the following year, he offered the story to editor Charles D. Hornig for his amateur magazine, *The Fantasy Fan*. It subsequently appeared in the March 1934 issue under the title 'Gods of the North'. Retaining its Hyborian Age setting, Howard rewrote the tale, replacing Conan with a similar hero named Amra of Akbitana.

The Conan variant remained unpublished for twenty years, until it was discovered amongst Howard's papers. 'The Frost-Giant's Daughter' finally saw print in the August 1953 issue of *Fantasy Fiction*, but in a version extensively revised by L. Sprague de Camp.

Having originally created the character for the unsold 'Marchers of Valhalla', 'The Garden of Fear' and four uncompleted stories, 'The Valley of the Worm' was another story about James Allison, who could remember past incarnations. In this tale, published in the February 1934 *Weird Tales*, the dying Allison returned to a previous life as Niord, a member of a nomadic tribe, where his battle against a giant subterranean creature became the basis of the dragon-slayer legend.

'The Garden of Fear' eventually appeared in the second issue of William L. Crawford's amateur publication, *Marvel Tales*, for July–August 1934. Unusually, the fanzine had two variant covers, only one of which heralded Howard's contribution. The story subsequently lent its title to a 1945 chapbook anthology, also edited and published by Crawford, which contained other reprint stories from *Marvel Tales* by L.A. Eshbach, H.P. Lovecraft, Miles J. Breuer, M.D. and David H. Keller, M.D.

With the publication of with 'The Phoenix on the Sword', Conan quickly became the author's most popular character, and Howard set his savage exploits in the Hyborian Age, a fictional period of pre-history "... which men have forgotten, but which remains in classical names, and distorted myths." He detailed Conan's world in a pseudo-historical essay entitled 'The Hyborian Age', which ran as a serial in Donald A. Wollheim's amateur magazine *The Phantagraph* in the issues dated February, August and October–November 1936. However, the fanzine only published the first half of the essay, and it finally appeared in its complete form as a mimeographed booklet in 1938.

According to his creator, Conan "... was born on a battle field, during a fight between his tribe and a horde of raiding Vanir. The country claimed by and roved over by his clan lay in the northwest of Cimmeria, but Conan was of mixed blood, although a pure-bred Cimmerian. His grandfather was a member of a southern tribe who had fled from his own people because of a blood-feud and after long wanderings, eventually taken refuge with the people of the north. He had taken part in many raids into the Hyborian nations in his youth, before his flight, and perhaps it was the tales he told of those softer countries which roused in Conan, as a child, a desire to see them.

"There are many things concerning Conan's life of which I am not certain myself. I do not know, for instance, when he got his first sight of civilized people. It might have been at Vanarium, or he might have made a peaceable visit to some frontier town before that. At Vanarium he was already a formidable antagonist, though only fifteen. He stood six feet and weighed 180 pounds, though he lacked much of having his full growth."

However, despite what Howard would claim later, the mighty-thewed barbarian did not leap fully-formed into his creator's mind. The June 1932 issue of *Strange Stories* contained Howard's story 'People of the Dark', whose hero was a warrior named Conan the reaver, who was physically similar to the later Conan and also swore "by Crom".

In fact, the first published Conan story, 'The Phoenix on the

Sword', is one of the final adventures in Conan's chronology, set after he had become king of Aquilonia. Wright conditionally accepted it in a letter dated March 10, 1932, describing it as having "... points of real excellence. I hope you will see your way clear to touch it up and resubmit it." It eventually appeared in the December 1932 issue of *Weird Tales* and was an instant hit, as indicated in the February 1933 edition of 'The Eyrie', where readers and writers alike were invited to air their comments and opinions about the magazine: "'The Phoenix on the Sword' fairly took my breath away with its fine intrigue and excellent action and description", exclaimed a reader from Denver, Colorado, adding: "It was a magnificent story. Mr. Howard never writes but that he produces a masterpiece."

This reworking of the unsold King Kull tale 'By This Axe I Rule!' finally saw print in its original form in the 1967 collection *King Kull*.

Still king of Aquilonia, Conan was ambushed and shackled in a dungeon, where he encountered an enormous serpent in 'The Scarlet Citadel', published in the January 1933 *Weird Tales*. Although Howard had already been awarded the coveted cover spot on previous issues of the magazine (his first had been for 'Wolfshead' back in April 1926), the covers for the December and January issues were two out of four which J. Allen St. John produced consecutively for Otis Adelbert Kline's serial 'Buccaneers of Venus'.

Howard also missed out on the cover for the March 1933 issue, which contained 'The Tower of the Elephant'. As Howard later explained in a letter to P. Schuyler Miller, "Conan was about seventeen when he was introduced to the public in 'The Tower of the Elephant'. While not fully matured, he was riper than the average civilized youth at that age." The author apparently borrowed the setting for the Zamorian thieves' quarter from one of his favourite movies, the 1923 version of *The Hunchback of Notre Dame*.

Conan led an army against a revived wizard in 'Black Colossus', his fourth adventure in *Weird Tales*, in the June 1933 issue. It also marked the first of nine cover appearances Howard's Conan series would make on the magazine.

Margaret Brundage's paintings were featured on most of the *Weird Tales* covers during the mid-1930s, and her cover for 'Black Colossus' depicted the naked Yasmela reaching out to touch the seated stone idol. A former Chicago fashion artist, Brundage was paid $90.00 per cover and usually worked in delicate pastel chalks on canvas. Wright admitted in the magazine that they had to be careful handling the artist's work: "The originals are so delicate that we are afraid even to sneeze when we have a cover design in our possession, for fear the picture will disappear in a cloud of dust."

"They were so impressed by the cover, that they brought it to the best engraver in Chicago," Brundage recalled. "Wright later told me that it generated the most mail ever for a cover for *Weird Tales*."

That was probably because her depictions of nude or diaphanously draped women, often in *risqué* or blatant bondage positions, provoked many outraged letters to 'The Eyrie'. However, Farnsworth Wright was a smart enough editor and businessman to note that issues which featured a Brundage nude on the cover invariably sold more copies on the newsstands!

In a letter to Clark Ashton Smith postmarked July 22, 1933, Howard told his fellow *Weird Tales* writer: "Thanks, too, for the kind things you said about Conan. I enjoy writing about him more than any character I have ever created. He almost seems to write himself. I find stories dealing with him roll out much easier than any others."

It was around this time that Robert E. Howard learned from E. Hoffman Price that Robert Hayward Barlow, a teenage protégé of Lovecraft's, was interested in publishing a possible collection of his Conan stories. "Price tells me that you are interested in the collection of first drafts of *Weird* stories," he wrote to Barlow. "I am sending by express, the first writings—or rather the first typings, since I do all my work on the typewriter—of 'The Phoenix on the Sword', 'The Scarlet Citadel', 'Black Colossus' and 'Iron Shadows in the Moon'. Some of the pages seem to be missing from the first named story, but the others are complete. Hoping you will find them of interest."

At the time, the last two stories had not yet appeared in *Weird Tales*, and when 'Iron Shadows in the Moon' finally appeared in the April 1934 issue of the magazine, Farnsworth Wright had retitled the novelette 'Shadows in the Moonlight'.

"He reeled away from the wall and met the leaping horror with a cast of his ax."

The
℘hoenix
on the Sword

By ROBERT E. HOWARD

A soul-searing story of a fearsome monster spawned in darkness before the first man crawled out of the slimy sea

Weird Tales

SEPT.

25c

NRA

THE PEOPLE OF THE BLACK CIRCLE

a smashing weird novel of eery black magic

By ROBERT E. HOWARD

SEABURY QUINN

GREYE LA SPINA

XI

*"Barbarism is the natural state of mankind.
Civilization is unnatural. It is a whim of
circumstance. And barbarism must always triumph."*
—Robert E. Howard

ORIGINALLY TITLED 'Xuthal of the Dusk', 'The Slithering Shadow' in the September 1933 *Weird Tales* found Conan in yet another lost city battling an evil Stygian witch and the toad-like god, Thog. The story was also featured on the cover with one of Brundage's most infamous "whipping" scenes. Future author Henry Kuttner commented in 'The Eyrie': "Allow me to pan you for your charmingly sadistic cover illustrating 'The Slithering Shadow'. I haven't the slightest objection to the female nude in art, but it seems rather a pity that it is possible to find such pictures in any sex magazine, while *Weird Tales* is about the only type of magazine which can run fantastic and weird cover illustrations and doesn't."

Conan joined up with a group of buccaneers in search of a treasure island in 'The Pool of the Black One' in the October 1933 issue of *Weird Tales*. In another letter to Clark Ashton Smith, postmarked December 14, 1933, Howard gave some more background to the creation of his most memorable character: "I'm rather of the opinion myself that widespread myths and legends are based on some fact, though the fact may be distorted out of all recognition in the telling...I know that for months I had been absolutely barren of ideas, completely unable to work up anything sellable. Then the man Conan seemed suddenly to grow up in my mind without much labor on my part and immediately a stream of stories flowed off my pen—or rather off my typewriter—almost without effort on my part. I did not seem to be creating, but rather relating events that had occurred. Episode crowded on episode so fast that I could scarcely keep up with them. For weeks I did nothing but write of the adventures of Conan. The character took complete possession of my mind and crowded out everything else in the way of story-writing. When I deliberately tried to write something else, I couldn't do it."

By now Howard's stories in the magazine were bringing him the same kind of popularity that such authors as Seabury Quinn and H.P. Lovecraft were also receiving in the letters column. In fact, except for Quinn's exploits of the psychic detective Jules de Grandin, Conan was the most popular character to ever appear in *Weird Tales*.

'Rogues in the House', which appeared in the January 1934 *Weird Tales*, was another of those Conan stories which seemed to write itself. This time, the young barbarian thief was saved from a dungeon by a nobleman seeking revenge. As Howard recalled: "I didn't rewrite it even once. As I remember I only erased and changed one word in it, and then sent it in just as it was written."

Perhaps that was why, in a letter to P. Schuyler Miller written in 1936, Howard admitted that even he was not absolutely certain of the background to his own story: "I am not sure that the adventure chronicled in 'Rogues in the House' occurred in Zamora. The presence of opposing factions of politics would seem to indicate otherwise, since Zamora was an absolute despotism where differing political opinions were not tolerated. I am of the opinion that the city was one of the small city-states lying just west of Zamora, and into which Conan had wandered after leaving Zamora. Shortly after this he returned for a brief period to Cimmeria, and there were other returns to his native land from time to time."

'Shadows in the Moonlight' in the April 1934 *Weird Tales* was the story originally given the title 'Iron Shadows in the Moon' by Howard. This time Conan and his female companion escaped from a battlefield slaughter and found themselves menaced by iron statues imbued with life by the rays of the full moon.

According to one reader from Rockdale, Texas, in the June 1934 issue: "As usual Conan provided some real thrills in Robert E. Howard's story, 'Shadows in the Moonlight'. In my humble opinion Conan is the greatest of WT's famous characters."

Conan fell in love with the female pirate Bêlit, leader of the Black Corsairs, in his next adventure. After keeping Conan off the cover for several issues, Wright used a Margaret Brundage painting for 'Queen of the Black Coast' on the May 1934 *Weird Tales*. It featured a delicate-looking Conan with a diaphanously draped damsel throwing her arms around his neck as he warded off a flying attacker with an ineffectual knife.

Meanwhile, the Brundage debate continued to rage in 'The Eyrie': "I do not think it would be at all an easy task to find anything to compare with Brundage's representations of sheer feminine loveliness without the touch of vulgarity and suggestiveness which usually accompany nudes in magazines," commented a male reader from El Paso, Texas, in the June 1934 issue, adding: "The cover illustrating 'Black Colossus' was about as beautiful a piece of art as I have seen in a long time."

However, in the same issue, a female reader from Oregon declared: "I do enjoy *Weird Tales* and usually manage to acquire one each month, even though I do tear off the cover immediately and stick it in the nearest receptacle for trash. Are such covers absolutely necessary?"

Like Farnsworth Wright, Robert E. Howard also knew his markets, and he knew how much he could get past his editor and still be certain of an eye-catching cover: "Another problem is how far you can go without shocking the readers into distaste for your stuff—and therefore cutting down sales... I don't know how much slaughter and butchery the readers will endure. Their capacity for grisly details seems unlimited, when the cruelty is the torturing of some naked girl. The torture of a naked writhing wretch, utterly helpless—and especially when of the feminine sex amid voluptuous surroundings—seems to excite keen pleasure in some people who have a distaste for wholesale butchery in the heat and fury of a battlefield."

Conan was the leader of a band of outlaws who battled a giant god of living metal in 'The Devil in Iron' in the August 1934 issue. It was the tenth Conan story to appear in *Weird Tales* and was voted by the readers as the best in that issue, despite another feeble Brundage cover depicting an unlikely-looking Conan entrapped by the coils of a giant green serpent while a semi-naked blonde looked on.

A much better Brundage cover was used for the first instalment of 'The People of the Black Circle', a three-part serial set in exotic north-west Asia which ran in the September, October and November 1934 issues of the magazine. This time the artist wisely ignored Conan in favour of the beautiful princess Yasmina being held in the clutches of an evil sorcerer.

This is how Wright introduced the serial to his readers: "Rough, and at times uncouth, Conan is a primitive man, who will brave almost certain death against terrific odds to rescue a damsel in distress; yet he will just as quickly give her a resounding slap on the posterior or drop her into a cesspool if she displeases him. But rude though he is, he possesses a sort of primordial chivalry and an innate reverence for womanhood that make him wholly fascinating."

Obviously the readers agreed, as this short novel was again voted the best story in the magazine and editor Wright revealed that "Robert E. Howard's spectacular and original hero, Conan the barbarian adventurer and fighting-man, has captured the fancy of our readers by his brilliant exploits and his utter humanness."

However, not everyone was so enamoured with the mighty Cimmerian. In the November 1934 *Weird Tales*, the following letter appeared in 'The Eyrie': "I am awfully tired of poor old Conan the Cluck, who for the past fifteen issues has every month slain a new wizard, tackled a new monster, come to a violent and sudden end that was averted (incredibly enough!) in just the nick of time, and won a new girl-friend, each of whose penchant for nudism won her place of honor, either on the cover or on the interior illustration... I cry: 'Enough of this brute and his iron-thewed sword-thrusts—may he be sent to Valhalla to cut out paper dolls.'" The author of this anti-Conan diatribe was none other than seventeen-year-old Robert Bloch, later to find lasting fame as the author of *Psycho*, whose own first professional sale, 'The Feast in the Abbey', would be appearing in the January 1935 edition of "The Unique Magazine".

When 'A Witch Shall Be Born', with its memorable crucifixion scene, was published in the December 1934 issue of *Weird Tales*, Brundage instead went for another of her suggestive "whipping" scenes on the cover, this time involving two near-naked women and a cat-o'-nine-tails.

Editor Farnsworth Wright's lengthy introduction announced that since Howard's first publication in the magazine back in 1925, "... he has had forty stories in *Weird Tales* alone, and has gained an enormous following among the readers of this magazine. Many thousands of readers eagerly buy any magazines that feature one of Mr. Howard's stories... He has the faculty of making real characters of his heroes, not mere automatons who act as they do merely because the author pulls the strings."

In early 1935 Howard's mother underwent a serious operation, remaining in hospital for a month before returning home. Novalyne Price Ellis later recalled meeting her: "Mrs. Howard was sitting on the end of a divan. Her hair was nearly white, short, and parted on one side, not stylish. It looked as if she just combed it quickly to get it over with, not to make her look better. She got up with a great effort and stood leaning slightly to one side."

Hester Howard never fully recovered her health, and she would spend the rest of her life visiting various hospitals and sanatoriums or being cared for at home by her husband and son.

'Jewels of Gwahlur' appeared in the March 1935 *Weird Tales*. It was a minor Conan tale, about the stealing of a cursed treasure from yet another lost city, which Howard had originally titled 'Teeth of Gwahlur'.

However, there was nothing minor about 'Beyond the Black River', the second of Conan's four serial-length appearances in *Weird Tales*, published in the May and June issues for 1935. Drawing upon its author's Texas background, it was a variation on the American frontier saga, with Howard's fictional Picts standing in for Native American warriors. It was also in this story that Howard had one of his characters famously observe: "Barbarism is the natural state of mankind. Civilization is unnatural. It is a whim of circumstance. And barbarism must always triumph." There is little doubt that the author was expressing his own views directly to the reader.

With 'Beyond the Black River' Howard was still experimenting with the series, as he revealed in a letter to H.P. Lovecraft: "I wanted to see if I could write an interesting Conan yarn without sex interest...I've attempted a new style of setting entirely— abandoned the exotic settings of lost cities, decaying civilizations, golden domes, marble palaces, silk-clad dancing girls, etc., and thrown my story against a background of forests and rivers, log cabins, frontier outposts, buckskin-clad settlers, and painted tribesmen."

It was around the same time that Howard also wrote but failed to sell 'Wolves Beyond the Border', which was set in the same milieu as 'Beyond the Black River' but did not feature Conan directly.

The May 1935 *Weird Tales* also included another letter from Robert Bloch, whose story 'The Secret of the Tomb' ran in the same issue: "I have been highly interested in the comments anent my so-called 'attack' on Howard in the Eyrie... At no time have I ever, directly or indirectly, maligned Mr. Howard's fine and obviously talented abilities as a writer; I confined myself solely to a criticism of Conan's career."

Meanwhile, the cost of Mrs. Howard's continued medical treatment and the effect it was having on his own practice was draining Dr. Howard's finances, and the family was in need of urgent cash.

At the time, *Weird Tales* still owed Howard more than $800 for stories which had already appeared and were supposedly paid for upon publication. In frustration, Howard wrote to Farnsworth Wright on May 6: "For some time now I have been receiving a check regularly each month from *Weird Tales*—half checks, it is true, but by practicing the most rigid economy I have managed to keep my head above the water; that I was able to do so was largely because of, not the size but the regularity of the checks. I came to depend upon them and to expect them, as I felt justified in so doing. But this month, at the very time when I need money so desperately bad, I did not receive a check. Somehow, some way, my family and I have struggled along this far, but if you cut off my monthly checks now, I don't know what in God's name we'll do...."

In an autobiographical sketch in the July 1935 issue of Julius Schwartz's amateur *Fantasy Magazine*, Howard told the readers: "Conan simply grew up in my mind a few years ago when I was stopping in a little border town on the lower Rio Grande. I did not create him by any conscious process. He simply stalked full grown out of oblivion and set me at work recording the saga of his adventures."

In a letter that same month to Clark Ashton Smith, Howard continued: "It may sound fantastic to link the term 'realism' with Conan; but as a matter of fact—his supernatural adventures aside—he is the most realistic character I ever evolved. He is simply a combination of a number of men I have known, and I think that's why he seemed to step full-grown into my consciousness when I wrote the first yarn of the series. Some mechanism in my subconsciousness took the dominant characteristics of various prize-fighters, gunmen, boot-leggers, oil field bullies, gamblers, and honest workmen I had come in contact with, and combining them all, produced the amalgamation I call Conan the Cimmerian."

Between the early months of 1932 and July 1935, Robert E. Howard wrote twenty-one adventures of Conan the barbarian. These tales varied in length from around 3,500 words to the almost novel-length of 75,000 words. Of these stories, seventeen were published in *Weird Tales*.

As the author explained: "Literature is a business to me—a business at which I was making an ample living when the Depression knocked the guts out of the markets. My sole desire in writing is to make a reasonable living. I may cling to many illusions, but I am not ridden by the illusion that I have anything wonderful or magical to say, or that it would amount to anything particularly if I did say it. I have no quarrel with art-for-art's-sakers. On the contrary, I admire their work. But my pet delusions tend in other directions."

Although Howard's writing career was improving again, his mother's fragile health was not. She had terminal tuberculosis. Also, as Novalyne Price Ellis later observed: "His mother had him so completely in her power that he hovered over her, even in a store. She was, of course, the only woman in his life."

Howard's idolisation of his mother would be his downfall. What neither knew was that time was quickly running out for both of them.

Gates of Empire

Giles . . . gripped the dazed king and dragged him clear.

by ROBERT E. HOWARD
Illustrated by HAROLD S. DELAY

XII

"Howard was my favourite author, I always
liked his stories best."
—Margaret Brundage

D ESPITE ENJOYING AN all-time high in sales during 1935
to such diverse pulp magazines as *Action Stories*, *Argosy*,
Dime Sports Magazine, *Spicy-Adventure Stories*, *Star Western*,
Thrilling Adventures, *Thrilling Mystery*, *Top-Notch*, *Western Aces*
and, of course, *Weird Tales*, Robert E. Howard had started talking
about taking his own life when it appeared that his mother was
dying.

As his father, Dr. I.M. Howard later recalled: "Last March a
year ago, again when his mother was very low in the King's
Daughters Hospital in Temple, Texas, Dr. McCelvey expressed a
fear that she would not recover; he began to talk to me about his
business, and I at once understood what it meant. I began to talk
to him, trying to dissuade him from such a course, but his mother
began to improve. Immediately she began to improve, he became
cheerful and no more was said."

Ignored or simply dismissed as eccentric by most of the
inhabitants of his hometown of Cross Plains, Texas, Howard began
to exhibit even more bizarre behaviour. He had told writer E.
Hoffman Price the previous year: "Nobody thinks I amount to

much, so I am proud to show these people that a successful writer thinks enough of me to drive a thousand miles to hell and gone out of his way to visit me."

Howard now decided to grow a long walrus moustache and walk around town dressed somewhat unconventionally, as Novalyne Price Ellis described in her memoir *One Who Walked Alone*: "The first thing that startled me was the black sombrero he had on. It was a real Mexican sombrero with little balls dangling from its rim. The chin strap was a thin little strip of leather attached to the hat. It came down and was tied under his chin. The vaqueros used the chin strap to keep their hats from being blown off by the incessant winds that swept the plains. But the flat crown and chin strap made Bob's face look rounder than ever . . . The red bandana around his neck was tied in the back. He didn't have on those old short, brown pants. Not this year! He had on short, *black* pants that came to the top of his black shoes."

In 'Shadows in Zamboula', which was published in the November 1935 issue of *Weird Tales*, Conan found himself staying in a city filled with intrigue and cannibalism. Howard's original title for the story had been 'The Man-Eaters of Zamboula'. The issue once again featured a Conan cover by Margaret Brundage, with a naked Nafertari surrounded by four hissing cobras. However, this time the story was closely beaten in the readers' poll by 'The Way Home' by Paul Frederick Stern (a pen-name for writer Paul Ernst).

At around 75,000 words, Howard's next entry in the series was twice as long as any other Conan story and Howard's only completed novel. Written over four months in the spring of 1934, he cannibalised and expanded a number of his earlier Conan stories—specifically 'The Scarlet Citadel', 'Black Colossus' and 'The Devil in Iron'—to create one of his finest and most mature works.

According to the author, "Conan was about forty when he seized the crown of Aquilonia, and was about forty-four or forty-five at the time of 'The Hour of the Dragon'. He had no male heir at that time, because he had never bothered to formally make some woman his queen, and the sons of concubines, of which he had a goodly number, were not recognized as heirs to the throne."

Howard had already had several stories reprinted between hardcovers in Britain in the *Not at Night* series of horror anthologies edited by Christine Campbell Thomson (including the Conan story 'Rogues in the House', which appeared in the 1934 volume *Terror at Night*). *The Hour of the Dragon* was submitted to British publisher Denis Archer in May 1934. The year before, Archer had turned down a collection of Howard's stories (which featured two Conan tales) with the suggestion that "any time you find yourself able to produce a full-length novel of about 70,000–75,000 words along the lines of the stories, my allied Company, Pawling & Ness Ltd, who deal with the lending libraries, and are able to sell a first edition of 5,000 copies, will be very willing to publish it."

In fact, Archer actually accepted *The Hour of the Dragon*, but the publisher went bankrupt and his assets, including Howard's novel, were put into the hands of the official receiver. The book was never published, and the story finally appeared as a five-part serial running in *Weird Tales* from December 1935 to April 1936 (with chapter 20 apparently mis-numbered as chapter 21).

Despite Margaret Brundage's cover depicting her most pathetic-looking Conan ever, chained in a cell while a scantily-clad Zenobia hands him the keys, readers reacted favourably to the serial in 'The Eyrie': "If 'The Hour of the Dragon' ends as good as it began I shall vote Mr. Howard your ace writer," promised a reader from Sioux City, Iowa. "Robert E. Howard's 'Hour of the Dragon' is vividly written, as are all Mr. Howard's stories," praised a reader from Hazleton, Pennsylvania, who continued: "Conan is at his bloodthirsty worst, killing off his enemies left and right; lovely damozels walk about in scanty shifts and pine to be held in his muscular arms—so what more could one want, I ask you?"

However, the Brundage controversy continued to rage: "I was greatly pleased with the stories in the December WT, but at the same time greatly disappointed with Mrs. Brundage's illustration of Conan," complained a reader from Washington D.C. "From Howard's stories I have always pictured Conan as a rough, muscular, scarred figure of giant stature with thick, wiry, black hair covering his massive chest, powerful arms, and muscular legs; and a face that's as rugged as the weather-beaten face of an old sea captain."

Howard expressed his own opinion of Margaret Brundage's work in a letter in the June 1936 issue: "Enthusiasm impels me to pause from burning spines off cactus for my drouth-bedeviled goats long enough to give three slightly dust-choked cheers for the April cover illustration . . . altogether I think it's the best thing Mrs. Brundage has done since she illustrated my 'Black Colossus'. And that's no depreciation of the covers done between these master-pictures."

"Howard was my favourite author," Brundage recalled many years later, "I always liked his stories best."

In terms of Conan's history, 'The Hour of the Dragon' (which was later reprinted under the title *Conan the Conqueror*) is the final story in the sequence. It was also the last Conan story Howard himself would ever see published.

XIII

"I believe I added as much to it as I borrowed."
—Clark Ashton Smith

I N 1933, Clark Ashton Smith self-published 1,000 copies of *The Double Shadow and Other Fantasies*, a thirty-page collection of six stories, which were amongst his favourites and which he was unable to sell at the time. He advertised copies in *The Fantasy Fan* for twenty-five cents each, "coin or stamps". In a letter dated March 15, 1933, Robert E. Howard thanked Smith for sending him a copy of the book: "I have read the stories with the most intense interest and appreciation, and hardly know which I like the best. All are magnificent, splendid examples of that poetic prose which is so characteristic of your work. I envy you your rich and vivid style". Yet, despite Howard's enthusiasm, as late as 1951 copies of *The Double Shadow* were still available directly from Smith for just $1.00 a copy.

Smith's story 'The White Sybil' was coupled with David H. Keller's story 'Men of Avalon' in the first booklet from William L. Crawford's Fantasy Publications in 1934, and late the following year, Smith began compiling a new collection of poems to be published by H.P. Lovecraft's young protégé Robert H. Barlow under the title *Incantations*. When Barlow's plans were delayed,

Smith's collection of ten poems entitled *Nero and Other Poems* appeared in May 1937 from Clyde Beck's The Futile Press in a printing of 150 copies. A month after publication, Beck had a further Smith poem and an essay by David Warren Ryder printed up on separate sheets and laid them into the remaining editions. Over the years several variant versions of this title have surfaced and the exact print run has never been determined.

In a 1935 letter, Howard praised Smith's poem 'Dominion' in the June *Weird Tales*: "I am not exaggerating when I say that I do not consider that I ever read a finer poem than that. I'd give my trigger-finger for the ability to make words flame and burn as you do".

Many of Smith's stories had been influenced by H.P. Lovecraft's tales of cosmic horror and, according to August Derleth, "none added so much as Clark Ashton Smith" to Lovecraft's famed interrelated series of stories known as the "Cthuhlu Mythos". "With consummate skill," continued Derleth, "Smith has added characters, enlarged on settings, spun his stories to embrace a far wider area in time for the Ancient Ones and the Elder Gods; he has himself invented the *Book of Eibon*, Tsathoggua, and many other place-names and characters in the Mythos, used by Lovecraft as well as himself."

Lovecraft himself observed: "None strikes the note of cosmic horror so well as Clark Ashton Smith... His stories deal powerfully with other galaxies, worlds and dimensions. Who else has seen such gorgeous, luxuriant, and feverishly distorted visions of infinite spheres and multiple dimensions and lived to tell the tale?"

According to at least one source, Smith published around twenty-six stories set in the Mythos. It was his tales of Hyperborea which the author described as "the closest to the Cthulhu Mythos, but most of them are written in a vein of grotesque humour that differentiates them vastly". Of these, the most important was probably 'The Tale of Satampra Zeiros', which the author considered one of his best. This story introduced the toad-god Tsathoggua, which was quickly appropriated by Lovecraft for his own pantheon of Old Ones.

"I believe I added as much to it as I borrowed," Smith later recalled about the Cthulhu Mythos.

"A fear which we had never experienced even in dreams deprived us of the faculty of speech."

THE TALE OF SATAMPRA ZEIROS

By CLARK ASHTON SMITH

A goose-flesh story of the horror that was consummated in the dark temple of the god Tsathoggua

I, SATAMPRA ZEIROS of Uzuldaroum, shall write with my left hand, since I have no longer any other, the tale of everything that befell Tirouv Ompallios and myself in the shrine of the god Tsathoggua, which lies neglected by the worship of man in the jungle-taken suburbs of Commoriom, that long-deserted capital of the Hyperborean rulers. I shall write it with the violet juice of the suvana-palm, which turns to a blood-red rubric with the passage of years, on a strong vellum that is made from the skin of the mastodon, as a warning to all good thieves and adventurers who may hear some lying legend of the lost treasures of Commoriom and be tempted thereby.

491

The CALL of CTHULHU
by H.P. LOVECRAFT

"The ring of worshipers moved in endless bacchanale between the ring of bodies and the ring of fire."

"Of such great powers or beings there may be conceivably a survival . . . a survival of a hugely remote period when . . . consciousness was manifested, perhaps, in shapes and forms long since withdrawn before the tide of advancing humanity . . . forms of which poetry and legend alone have caught a flying memory and called them gods, monsters, mythical beings of all sorts and kinds. . . ."
—*Algernon Blackwood.*

1. The Horror in Clay.

THE most merciful thing in the world, I think, is the inability of the human mind to correlate all its contents. We live on a placid island of ignorance in the midst of black seas of infinity, and it

Found among the papers of the late Francis Wayland Thurston, of Boston.

was not meant that we should voyage far. The sciences, each straining in its own direction, have hitherto harmed us little; but some day the piecing together of dissociated knowledge will open up such terrifying vistas of reality, and of our frightful position therein, that we shall either go mad from the revelation or flee from the deadly light into the peace and safety of a new dark age.

Theosophists have guessed at the awesome grandeur of the cosmic cycle wherein our world and human race form transient incidents. They have hinted at strange survivals in terms which would freeze the blood if not masked by a bland optimism.

XIV

"All my stories, unconnected as they may be, are based on
the fundamental lore or legend that this world was
inhabited at one time by another race who, in practising
Black Magic, lost their foothold and were expelled, yet live
outside, ever ready to take possession of this earth again".
—Attributed to H.P. Lovecraft by August Derleth

H IS CREATION OF a loosely connected group of works
which later came to be called the Cthulhu Mythos is
perhaps H.P. Lovecraft's most outstanding literary accomplish-
ment, and arguably his enduring claim to fame.

However, it would be true to say that a central theme had never
been in Lovecraft's mind while writing any of his tales. The famous
quote attributed to Lovecraft by August Derleth—"All my stories,
unconnected as they may be, are based on the fundamental lore
or legend that this world was inhabited at one time by another race
who, in practising Black Magic, lost their foothold and were
expelled, yet live outside, ever ready to take possession of this earth
again"—actually came from a correspondent of the author's, Dr.
Harold S. Farnese, who appears to have had a habit of accidentally
misremembering some of the things Lovecraft said in his letters.

The first major story in this sequence, 'The Nameless City', was
written in January 1921 and included the first references to the
mad poet, Abdul Alhazred, which also happened to be a childhood
pseudonym of Lovecraft's.

Although the so-called Cthulhu Mythos consisted of a number

of stories unrelated in characters, setting or period, they shared a common background of mythological lore. However, Lovecraft was a supreme rationalist and an avowed atheist. His Mythos therefore mostly eschewed the supernatural in favour of a scientific rationale. Rejecting the old-fashioned monsters of Gothic horror, he made his ancient gods sentient creatures from distant worlds, dimensions or other planes of existence.

As Ramsey Campbell has noted: "August Derleth sought to codify Lovecraft's inventions by reducing their activities to a standard occult struggle, and misrepresenting Cthulhu as a water elemental!"

In Derleth's sanitised version of Lovecraft's Mythos, millions of years ago, they came down from the stars and dominated the Earth. Utilising the classic conflict of Good vs. Evil, Derleth's interpretation of Lovecraft's deities is of two different natures: the nameless Old Ones or Ancient Ones, also known as the Elder Gods, personify the forces of cosmic good. Their adversaries, who are called by many names, are apparently representative of the four elements. Aeons ago, the Old Ones banished these Evil Ones. Now they wait hidden in the depths of the oceans, imprisoned on distant worlds, or lurk in the spaces beyond time. However, their malign influence remains in frightful myths of ancient antiquity and they are worshipped with loathsome rites by elder cults in remote backwaters. Although the Old Ones continue to keep these evil entities in check, there is a fear that they may one day awake from their deathless sleep, break their bonds and . . . *return!*

"These Great Old Ones were not composed altogether of flesh and blood," Lovecraft revealed in his seminal 1926 novellette 'The Call of Cthulhu': "They had shape, but that shape was not made of matter. When the stars were right, They could plunge from world to world through the sky; but when the stars were wrong, They could not live. But although They no longer lived, They could never really die."

When originally submitted to *Weird Tales*, editor Farnsworth Wright initially rejected the story. "I read the typescript and thought it as fine a narrative as he [Lovecraft] had yet written," wrote Donald Wandrei. "He too had thought well of it, but he said Wright had rejected it on the grounds that readers would not understand it, and he was plainly discouraged."

After talking with Wandrei, who had (deceptively) claimed that Lovecraft was planning to submit the story to other magazines, Wright asked to see the manuscript again and bought it for $165.00. It appeared in the February 1928 issue.

"Mr. Lovecraft's latest story, 'The Call of Cthulhu', is indeed a masterpiece, which I am sure will live as one of the highest achievements of literature," gushed Robert E. Howard in 'The Eyrie'.

In his 26,000-word novelette 'The Whisperer in Darkness', first published in the August 1931 issue of *Weird Tales*, Lovecraft famously listed the names of many of his Evil Ones and places connected with them:

"I found myself faced by names and terms that I had heard elsewhere in the most hideous of connections—Yuggoth, Great Cthulhu, Tsathoggua, Yog-Sothoth, R'lyeh, Nyarlathotep, Azathoth, Hastur, Yian, Leng, the Lake of Hali, Bethmoora, the Yellow Sign, L'mur-Kathulos, Bran, and the Magnum Innominandum—and was drawn back through nameless aeons and inconceivable dimensions to worlds of elder, outer entity at which the crazed author of the *Necronomicon* had only guessed in the vaguest way."

(It is perhaps worth noting here that the author suggested pronouncing the name "Cthulhu" as "Clutu", with both "u"s long, according to his friend W. Paul Cook although, according to Donald Wandrei, on another occasion Lovecraft vocalised it as "K-Lütl-Lütl" and Robert H. Barlow claimed he pronounced it as "Koot-u-lew".)

Lovecraft's stories are filled with allusions to and authentic-sounding quotations from obscure books and manuscripts, as he used references to fictional tomes of eldritch lore (often borrowed from the work of other writers, such as Lord Dunsany, Ambrose Bierce, Robert W. Chambers, Clark Ashton Smith and Robert E. Howard) to create the illusion of authenticity. His Mythos tales are filled with scholarly mentions of such works as old Ludwig Prinn's hellish *De Vermis Mysteriis*, the infamous *Cultes des Goules* of the Comte d'Erlette, the sinister *Liber Ivonis* and—perhaps most infamous of all—the forbidden Latin version of the abhorred *Necronomicon* by the mad Arab, Abdul Alhazred.

"After his first tales," explained August Derleth, somewhat controversially, "there began to develop in his later ones a curious coherence, a myth pattern so convincing that readers began to explore libraries and museums for certain imaginary titles of Lovecraft's own creation."

According to author and editor Lin Carter, "To further seduce his readers into a momentary suspension of disbelief, Lovecraft buttressed his fictional creations by surrounding them with an elaborate machinery of invented sources—learned anthropological allusions, data drawn from the literature of archaeology, spurious quotations from rare texts of ancient lore. To baffle and intrigue, he cleverly mingled fact with fiction, scholarship with invention; references to the mysterious Ponape ruins, to the enigmatic stone colossi of Easter Island, and jungle-grown remnants of antique Mayan civilizations appear cheek by jowl with whispered hints of 'cyclopean and many-columned Y'ha-nthlei', 'sunken R'lyeh in the Pacific' and 'fabulous Irem, City of Pillars, in Arabia Deserta.'"

To add to the confusion and fascination of his readers, Lovecraft cleverly intermingled his allusions to purely imaginary books with references to such actual titles as Murray's *Witch-Cult in Western Europe* and Frazer's *The Golden Bough*. He also set a number of his stories in a fictional area of Massachusetts, centred around the valley of the Miskatonic and the fictional towns of

Kingsport, Innsmouth, Dunwich and Arkham (first mentioned in 'The Festival').

"To an extent his reputation is the victim of his most famous creation, the Lovecraft Mythos," explained Ramsey Campbell. "It was conceived as an antidote to conventional Victorian occultism—as an attempt to reclaim the imaginative appeal of the unknown—and is only one of many ways his tales suggest worse, or greater, than they show."

Given their continued popularity and influence on modern horror fiction, it is perhaps surprising to discover that, of all H.P. Lovecraft's stories, only around a dozen or so can actually be considered to form the core of the Cthulhu Mythos.

The earliest tale which is acknowledged as genuinely belonging in the Mythos is the dream-inspired 'The Nameless City', which was written in January 1921. The last, 'The Haunter of the Dark', was written in November 1935, two years before the author's death. In between, he expanded his inter-connected mythology with such tales as 'The Festival' (written in October, 1923), 'The Call of Cthulhu' (Summer, 1926), 'The Case of Charles Dexter Ward' (January–March, 1927), 'The Colour Out of Space' (March, 1927), 'The Dunwich Horror' (Summer, 1928), 'The Whisperer in Darkness' (February–September, 1930), 'At the Mountains of Madness' (February–March, 1931), 'The Shadow Over Innsmouth' (November–December, 1931), 'The Dreams in the Witch-House' (January–February, 1932), 'The Thing on the Doorstep' (August, 1933) and 'The Shadow Out of Time' (November, 1934–March, 1935).

Over the years, the number of Lovecraft stories that actually comprise the Cthulhu Mythos has been vehemently debated by various researchers and continues to provoke discussion to this day.

"As a matter of record," August Derleth stated in the mid-1940s, "there is everything to show that Lovecraft had no intention whatsoever of evolving his Cthulhu Mythos until that pattern made itself manifest in his work; this explanation alone would account for certain trivial inconsistencies."

The initial grouping of Mythos stories by Lovecraft were added to and developed by an ever-widening circle of writers. It has been argued that Lovecraft did not actively encourage these pastiches, although at first they were mostly written by his correspondents and fellow writers from *Weird Tales*. It was also Lovecraft's habit to adopt the inventions of his friends—such as the names of demonic divinities, exotic locations and cursed volumes—and give them his "seal of approval" by then incorporating them into his own stories.

As a result, Clark Ashton Smith's *Book of Eibon*, Robert E. Howard's *Unaussprechlichen Kulten* by Friedrich Wilhelm von Junzt, Frank Belknap Long, Jr's translation of the *Necronomicon* by Dr. John Dee, and August Derleth's *Cultes des Goules* by the Comte d'Erlette were all added to the shelf of terrifying tomes of eldritch lore.

"He was, in reality, a kind, considerate, courteous man," recalled Robert Bloch, who began corresponding with Lovecraft when he was just fifteen years old, "generous to a fault with his time and talent." In his 1935 *Weird Tales* story 'The Shambler from the Stars', Bloch featured a thinly disguised Lovecraft as his doomed New England protagonist.

"Naturally I had written to Mr. Lovecraft, asking if I could use him as a character and, incidentally, kill him off," Bloch explained in his "unauthorised" 1993 autobiography, *Once Around the Bloch*. "He not only agreed but also sent me an official note of permission signed by a number of *his* Cthulhu Mythos characters."

However, the following year, Lovecraft took his revenge by killing off Milwaukee writer "Robert Blake" in his tale 'The Haunter of the Dark'. "Lovecraft dedicated it to me," continued Bloch, "—the only story of his ever bearing a dedication—and for this I am forever grateful."

In the September 1950 issue of *Weird Tales*, the author completed the three-story sequence with 'The Shadow from the Steeple', in which fellow writer Fritz Leiber ended up as the unfortunate victim.

Despite his growing fame (albeit amongst a small literary circle dedicated to a mostly-disregarded genre), Lovecraft continued to provide a literary revision service as a method of subsidising his meagre income from writing. It was through this service of extensively revising the work of some of his less talented clients that Lovecraft added stories by such writers as Frank Belknap Long, Hazel Heald, William Lumley and Zealia Bishop to the Cthulhu Mythos.

In fact, Bishop felt so grateful to Lovecraft that when her story 'Medusa's Coil' ultimately appeared in the January 1939 issue of *Weird Tales*, she stipulated that half the fee ($120.00) should be paid to his surviving aunt, Annie E.P. Gamwell. "My debt to Lovecraft is great," she admitted. "I count myself fortunate that I was one of his epistolary friends and pupils."

In 1935, Lovecraft contributed the middle section to a 6,000-word round-robin story, 'The Challenge from Beyond', published in the September issue of *Fantasy Magazine*, an amateur publication produced by New York fan Julius Schwartz. The other chapters were written by C.L. Moore, A. Merritt, Frank Belknap Long and Robert E. Howard.

XV

"I don't want to live to be old. I want to die when my time comes, quickly and suddenly, in the full tide of my strength and health."

—Robert E. Howard

ROBERT E. HOWARD was still upset over his mother's failing health, as his father later revealed: "Again this year, in February, while his mother was very sick and not expected to live but a few days, at that time she was in the Shannon Hospital in San Angelo, Texas. San Angelo is something like one hundred miles from here. He was driving back and forth daily from San Angelo to home. One evening he told me I would find his business, what little there was to it, all carefully written up and in a large envelope in his desk."

In a letter to Novalyne Price Ellis dated February 14, 1936, Howard admitted: "You ask how my mother is getting along. I hardly know what to say. Some days she seems to be improving a little, and other days she seems to be worse. I frankly don't know."

Conan's final appearance in *Weird Tales* was the three-part serial 'Red Nails' in the July, August–September and October 1936 issues. Howard described it as "... the grimmest, bloodiest and most merciless story of the series so far. Too much raw meat, maybe, but I merely portrayed what I honestly believe would be the reactions of certain types of people in the situations on which the plot of the story hung."

In a letter dated December 5, 1935, he called it "...the bloodiest and most sexy weird story I ever wrote. I have been dissatisfied with my handling of decaying races in stories, for the reason that degeneracy is so prevalent in such races that even in fiction it can not be ignored as a motive and as a fact if the fiction is to have any claim to realism. I have ignored it in all other stories, as one of the taboos, but I did not ignore it in this story. When, or if, you ever read it, I'd like to know how you like my handling of the subject of lesbianism."

In fact, there is only the slightest suggestion of lesbianism in the published version of the story, in which Conan and beautiful Aquilonian mercenary Valeria discovered yet another lost city and battled a monster reptile.

Introducing 'Red Nails' in the July 1936 issue, editor Farnsworth Wright recalled: "Nearly four years ago, *Weird Tales* published a story called 'The Phoenix on the Sword' built around a barbarian adventurer named Conan, who had become king of a country by sheer force of valor and brute strength... The stories of Conan were speedily acclaimed by our readers, and the barbarian's weird adventures became immensely popular. The story presented herewith is one of the most powerful and eery [*sic*] weird tales yet written about Conan. We commend this story to you, for we know you will enjoy it through and through."

Margaret Brundage's suggestive cover depicted a naked Valeria about to be sacrificed on an altar by three seductive slave girls. It was the last illustration Brundage would do for a Howard story and with the next issue of *Weird Tales* she ended her continuous run of thirty-nine covers for "The Unique Magazine". She would still occasionally make an appearance on the cover over the next nine years, and her final original painting—her sixty-sixth—appeared on the January 1945 issue.

Written in July 1935, 'Red Nails' was not only the final Conan story, but the final fantasy story that Robert E. Howard would complete. With his mother's hospital bills escalating, and *Weird Tales* (supposedly) paying on publication some of the lowest rates in the pulp field, he began to look around for better and more dependable markets. As he revealed in a letter dated February 15, 1936, to E. Hoffman Price: "For myself, I haven't submitted anything to *Weird Tales* for many months, though I would, if payments could be made a little more promptly. I reckon the boys have their troubles, same as me, but my needs are urgent and immediate."

Price observed that during his 1934 visit to Cross Plains: "I had often got the impression that Robert was a parent to his parents; that while he could have done the gypsying which other authors permitted themselves, solicitude for his father and mother kept him fairly close to home."

Novalyne Price Ellis agreed: "I do think Bob has tried to take over his parents' lives. He said once that parents and children change places in life. When parents become old and sick, you take care of them as you would a child."

During the spring of 1936, Hester Howard appeared to grow stronger, much to the relief of her son, as Dr. Howard later explained: "He accepted her condition as one of permanent improvement and one that would continue. I knew well that it would not, but I kept it from him."

In a letter written to August Derleth, dated May 9, 1936, Howard offered his own thoughts after recent deaths in Derleth's family: "Death to the old is inevitable, and yet somehow I often feel that it is a greater tragedy than death to the young. When a man dies young he misses much suffering, but the old have only life as a possession and somehow to me the tearing of a pitiful remnant from weak old fingers is more tragic than the looting of a life in its full rich plume. I don't want to live to be old. I want to die when my time comes, quickly and suddenly, in the full tide of my strength and health."

In a letter dated May 13, he also confided to H.P. Lovecraft that he did not know whether his mother would: "...live or not. She is very weak and weighs only 109 pounds—150 pounds is her normal weight—and very few kinds of food agree with her; but if she does live, she will owe her life to my father's efforts."

For three weeks Robert E. Howard continued to maintain an almost constant vigil at his beloved mother's bedside as her condition began to decline rapidly. Atypically, his mood became almost cheerful, as if he had finally made up his mind about something.

Then, on the morning of June 11, 1936, Howard learned from one of two trained nurses attending Mrs. Howard that his mother had entered a terminal coma and that she would probably never recognise him again. He rose from beside her sick-bed, slipped out of the house, climbed into his 1935 Chevrolet sedan parked in front of the garage and rolled up the windows. At a few minutes past eight o'clock in the morning, he fired a single bullet from a borrowed Colt .380 automatic into his right temple. He had come to the decision that he would not see his mother die.

The bullet passed through his brain and he survived for eight hours in a coma. He was thirty years old. His mother died shortly after ten o'clock on the evening of the following day, without ever regaining consciousness. She was sixty-six (although she had claimed to be several years younger). They were buried in adjacent graves in identical caskets at Brownwood's Greenleaf Cemetery.

A strip of paper was discovered after Howard shot himself. It contained two typewritten lines taken from Viola Garvin's poem 'The House of Cæsar':

> *All fled—all done, so lift me on the pyre—*
> *The Feast is over and the lamps expire.*

Having pretty much ignored him for most of his life, on the

day of his death the local newspaper reprinted one of Howard's last Western stories, along with a 6,000-word article and an obituary—more space than any citizen of Cross Plains had ever received.

On June 24, 1936, Howard's beloved library of some 300 books and file copies of all the magazines which contained his stories were donated by his father to Howard Payne College to form The Robert E. Howard Memorial Collection. Nine months later Dr. Howard reclaimed all his son's magazines because they were falling apart.

In a letter dated June 29, 1936, Dr. Howard wrote to H.P. Lovecraft: "... Robert was a great admirer of you. I have often heard him say that you were the best weird writer in the world, and he keenly enjoyed corresponding with you. Often expressed hope that you might visit in our home some day, so that he, his mother and I might see and know you personally. Robert greatly admired all weird writers, often heard him speak of each separately and express the highest admiration of all. He said they were a bunch of great men and he admired all of them very much."

Lovecraft's own 'Robert Ervin Howard: A Memoriam' was published in the September 1936 issue of Julius Schwartz's *Fantasy Magazine*:

> The character and attainments of Mr. Howard were wholly unique. He was, above everything else, a lover of the simpler, older world of barbarian and pioneer days, when courage and strength took the place of subtlety and stratagem, and when a hardy, fearless race battled and bled, and asked no quarter from hostile nature. All his stories reflect this philosophy, and derive from it a vitality found in few of his contemporaries. No one could write more convincingly of violence and gore than he, and his battle passages reveal an instinctive aptitude for military tactics which would have brought him distinction in times

of war. His real gifts were even higher than the readers of his published works would suspect, and had he lived, would have helped him to make his mark in serious literature with some folk epic of his beloved southwest... Always a disciple of hearty and strenuous living, he suggested more than casually his own famous character—the intrepid warrior, adventurer, and seizer of thrones, Conan the Cimmerian. His loss at the age of thirty is a tragedy of the first magnitude, and a blow from which fantasy fiction will not soon recover.

While writing those words, Lovecraft could hardly have realised that the world of fantasy fiction would soon be mourning the impact of his own premature death, at the age of forty-seven, little more than nine months later.

"The horror collapsed and rolled down the steps, as dead as the witch who had summoned it."

HUGH RANKIN

A Witch Shall Be Born
By ROBERT E. HOWARD

COMING NEXT MONTH

ROBERT E. HOWARD, at the time of his tragic death, was working on a new novel for WEIRD TALES. He had completed a rough first draft, and nearly completed a revision which was to be his final version. The bullet which crashed into his brain prevented the author from finishing this, his last story. It is a thrilling tale of popping action, depicted as only Howard could depict action, with a bone-crushing wildcat of a hero, in the weirdest possible adventures.

So engrossing is this story, *Almuric*, that WEIRD TALES would not be playing fair with you, the readers, if we did not let you see it. Therefore we have pieced together the nearly completed final draft that Howard wrote, with the final pages of Howard's rough first draft, which contains a smashing denouement.

Beginning in the United States in our day, the scene quickly shifts to another planet, called by the author Almuric. From his arrival in Almuric, the hero tells the story of his weird adventures in his own words. And what adventures they are! The creator of those indomitable characters that have delighted thousands of readers of this magazine—King Kull and his Shadow Kingdom, Solomon Kane the dour Puritan righter of wrongs, Conan the barbarian adventurer—has here created the doughtiest hero of them all: Esau Cairn, also known as Esau Ironhand.

This fascinating story will begin publication in next month's WEIRD TALES.

ALMURIC
By Robert E. Howard

—also—

THE DARK ISLE
By ROBERT BLOCH

A tale of the Romans and the Druids, and the horrendous doom revealed by the flaring torchlight in a frightful underground cavern in England.

THE THINKING MACHINE
By J. J. CONNINGTON

A strange and curious story about a fantastic machine that possessed a brute desire to slay—a startling thrill-tale of an eery invention.

THE HOLLOW MOON
By EVERIL WORRELL

A fascinatingly different story about a weird adventure that befell a yachting party shipwrecked in the South Seas—the strangest of all vampire tales.

WASHINGTON NOCTURNE
By SEABURY QUINN

Who was the stranger that walked before the Tomb and vanished, yet by his mere coming radically changed the lives of three persons?—a tale of the Unknown Soldier.

May Issue of Weird Tales . . . . . Out April 1

XVI

"An even greater irony was the commercial success of
Howard's writings thirty-odd years after his death."
—L. Sprague de Camp

ROBERT E. HOWARD'S father continued to correspond with
E. Hoffman Price until he died, a lonely old man suffering
from diabetes and cataracts in both eyes, on November 12, 1944.
As Price later recalled: "Whenever I think of Dr. Howard, well into
his seventy-fourth year, and with failing eyesight, having for these
past eight years faced alone and single handed a home and a world
from which both wife and son were taken in one day, I can not help
but say, 'I wish Robert had had more of his father's courage.'"

The notice of Robert E. Howard's death appeared in the
August–September issue of *Weird Tales*:

As this issue goes to press, we are saddened by the news of
the sudden death of Robert E. Howard of Cross Plains,
Texas. Mr. Howard for years has been one of the most
popular magazine authors in the country... It was in
Weird Tales that the cream of his writing appeared. Mr.
Howard was one of our literary discoveries... Prolific
though he was, his genius shone through everything he
wrote and he did not lower his high literary standards for
the sake of mere volume.

At the time, the magazine still owed Howard $1,350 for stories it had already published.

Regular *Weird Tales* cover artist Margaret Brundage remembered how she learned of the author's death: "I came into the offices one day and Wright informed me of Howard's suicide. We both just sat around and cried for most of the day. He was always my personal favourite."

Robert Bloch, who had previously criticised Howard's Conan stories in the magazine wrote: "Robert E. Howard's death is quite a shock—and a severe blow to WT. Despite my standing opinion of Conan, the fact always remains that Howard was one of WT's finest contributors."

Although it is true that Robert E. Howard never wrote or published the Conan stories in any particular sequence, in a letter dated March 10, 1936 to science fiction writer P. Schuyler Miller, the author responded to an attempt by Miller and chemist Dr. John D. Clark to put the Conan series into chronological order with his own concept of Conan's eventual fate: "Frankly I can't predict it. In writing these yarns I've always felt less as creating them than as if I were simply chronicling his adventures as he told them to me. That's why they skip about so much, without following a regular order. The average adventurer, telling tales of a wild life at random, seldom follows any ordered plan, but narrates episodes widely separated by space and years, as they occur to him."

The Cimmerian's adventures appeared as the author imagined them—consequently the first two stories published, 'The Phoenix on the Sword' and 'The Scarlet Citadel', feature an older Conan who has already been crowned king of Aquilonia, while the character appears as a teenage thief in the third published tale, 'The Tower of the Elephant'.

One explanation for this apparently random chronology appears in a letter postmarked December 14, 1933 to Clark Ashton Smith, in which Howard hinted at a possible preternatural power behind the creation of his character: "While I don't go so far as to believe that stories are inspired by actually existent spirits or powers (though I am rather opposed to flatly denying anything) I have sometimes wondered if it were possible that unrecognized forces of the past or present—or even the future—work through the thoughts and actions of living men. This occurred to me when I was writing the first stories of the Conan series especially... I do not attempt to explain this by esoteric or occult means, but the facts remain. I still write of Conan more powerfully and with more understanding than any of my other characters. But the time will probably come when I will suddenly find myself unable to write convincingly of him at all. That has happened in the past with nearly all my rather numerous characters; suddenly I would find myself out of contact with the conception, as if the man himself had been standing at my shoulder directing my efforts, and had suddenly turned and gone away, leaving me to search for another character."

Despite his premature death, Robert E. Howard's stories continued to appear in the pulp magazines. These were either submitted before his death, or subsequently discovered amongst the author's papers.

Written under the title 'The Road of the Mountain Lion' and originally announced as "forthcoming" in the final, January 1934 issue of *The Magic Carpet Magazine*, 'Gates of Empire' eventually saw publication in the historical adventure magazine *Golden Fleece* in January 1939.

Possibly written at the urging of his agent, Otis Adelbert Kline—who had himself produced a number of works in a similar vein—Howard's short novel 'Almuric' was very much in the style of Edgar Rice Burroughs' popular planetary romances set on Mars or Venus. It is known that Howard admired Burroughs' work and had a number of the author's books in his library.

"Robert E. Howard, at the time of his tragic death, was working on a new novel for *Weird Tales*," it was claimed in the April 1939 issue of the magazine. In fact, it was more likely that Howard had intended to submit 'Almuric' to a better-paying market such as *Argosy*, or to the British book publisher who had expressed interest in his work.

"He had completed a rough draft and nearly completed a revision which was to be his final version," continued the announcement. "We have pieced together the nearly completed final draft that Howard wrote, with the final pages of Howard's rough first draft, which contains a smashing denouement."

Probably written around 1934, and left in first and partial second drafts to be revised by the author later, it has been speculated that either Kline or writer Otto Binder may have had a hand in editing and completing the manuscript after it was submitted to *Weird Tales* following Howard's death.

Editor Farnsworth Wright paid Kline $375 for 'Almuric' and ran it as a three-part serial in the May, June–July and August 1939 issues, with illustrations by the peerless Virgil Finlay.

"Let me say right now that 'Almuric' is about the best and most unusual of any Howard story I've read," enthused a letter-writer to 'The Eyrie'. "We still lament the loss of so fine a writer—so brilliant a brain. Esau Cairn of Almuric is quite some fellow—the illustrations really bring him wonderfully to life."

"To say that I merely enjoyed 'Almuric' would be a gross understatement," announced another correspondent, "for I visited there an alien world, fought back-to-back with the strongest man on two planets, suffered the cold of the peril-fraught night. Surely, no mean author it is who can thus gain such absolute control over the subconscious of his readers."

It was therefore no surprise when the readers of *Weird Tales* voted the first instalment of 'Almuric' the most popular story in that issue.

E. Hoffman Price estimated that (excluding reprints), between

July 1925 and August 1939, sixty-four stories by Howard were published in the pages of *Weird Tales, Oriental Stories* and *The Magic Carpet Magazine*. This total included seven serials and, overall, Howard appeared in seventy-eight issues of those magazines. Of course, that does not include all his contributions to other markets during the same period.

Although a number of his stories—mostly pseudonymous Westerns—and some poems continued to be published over the next decade, it was not until the early 1950s that Howard's work became popular again. This was in no small way due to the Gnome Press collections of Conan and L. Sprague de Camp's posthumous "collaborations".

"An even greater irony was the commercial success of Howard's writings thirty-odd years after his death," recalled de Camp. "But of course he had no way of foreseeing that."

"Again and again I saw a winged man soar up through the whirling smoke, gripping a shrieking girl in his arms."

Almuric

By ROBERT E. HOWARD

XVII

"Everything I loved had been dead for two centuries.
I am never a part of anything around me—in
everything I am an outsider."

—H.P. Lovecraft

ALTHOUGH H.P. LOVECRAFT had enjoyed some success
with 'At the Mountains of Madness' and 'The Shadow Out
of Time' appearing in *Astounding Stories* in 1936 (both of which
were sold on his behalf by other people), the author continued to
treat the marketing of his own work with almost careless abandon.

When he had submitted his first five stories to Edwin Baird at
Weird Tales back in 1923, Lovecraft had made the amateurish
mistake of telling him that he paid "no attention to the demands of
commercial writing", which must have been music to the ears of an
editor constrained by budgets and late payments to authors. And
the author continued to complain to friends about "the vulgar
necessity of financial striving".

Stories such as 'From Beyond' (written in November, 1920)
and 'The Quest of Iranon' (written in February, 1921) made their
initial appearances in fan publications for little or no money.
Although two new stories, 'Through the Gates of the Silver Key'
(written with E. Hoffmann Price, October. 1932–April, 1933) and
'The Haunter of the Dark' (written November 5–9, 1935), both saw
their first publication in *Weird Tales*, editor Farnsworth Wright was

forced to keep those readers clamouring for more Lovecraft fiction appeased with reprints of such previously-published tales as 'The White Ape', 'Dagon', 'The Temple' and 'Pickman's Model', amongst others.

Written in August 1933, 'The Thing on the Doorstep' was another original Lovecraft story that Wright published in the January 1937 issue of *Weird Tales*. What neither of them could have foreseen at the time was that it would be the author's last new story to appear in the magazine prior to his death.

In 1934, Lovecraft had begun to complain about suffering from "indigestion" or "grippe". In fact, he had a combination of colon cancer and Bright's disease (which affects the kidneys). However, he did not consult a doctor until more than two years after he first noticed the symptoms, by which time his illness was already inoperable.

He became weaker and had trouble eating food, resulting in a marked loss of weight. That Lovecraft probably suspected the nature of his illness is revealed in a letter he sent to August Derleth in February 1937, writing about his renewed interest in astronomy: "Funny how early interests crop up again toward the end of one's life".

Howard Phillips Lovecraft died at the age of forty-six on the morning of March 15, 1937 at the Jane Brown Memorial Hospital. He was buried in the family plot in the Swan Point Cemetery three days later, where his name was inscribed alongside those of his parents. A handful of people attended the funeral service.

"Everything I loved had been dead for two centuries," Lovecraft wrote in 1916. "I am never a part of anything around me—in everything I am an outsider...But pray do not think, gentlemen, that I am an utterly forlorn and misanthropick creature...Despite my solitary life, I have found infinite joy in books and writing, and am by far too much interested in the affairs of the world to quit the scene before Nature shall claim me...A sense of humour has helped me to endure existence; in fact, when all else fails, I never fail to extract a sarcastic smile from the contemplation of my own empty and egotistical career...!"

What Lovecraft could not possibly have predicted was that, so far as his popularity as a writer was concerned, like his friend Robert E. Howard it would only be after his untimely death that his career would really begin to take off...

More than eighty-five years after his death, H.P. Lovecraft remains one of the most important and influential authors of supernatural fiction. This, despite the fact that he was never widely published during his lifetime, except in the pages of amateur journals, specialist pulp magazines such as *Weird Tales*, and in a few hardcover anthologies of horror stories.

The only book of his fiction Lovecraft lived to see published during his lifetime was *Shadow Over Innsmouth* (1936). A slender 26,000-word novelette illustrated with four pieces of artwork by Frank A. Utpatel, it was produced by William L. Crawford's Visionary Publishing Company of Everett, Pennsylvania.

"Crawford has at last issued my 'Innsmouth' as a lousily misprinted and sloppily bound book," the author complained in a letter. "The printed errata slip doesn't cover half the mistakes."

Although Crawford managed to produce around 400 copies, only half of these were bound in hardcovers. He sold just 150 copies before he was forced to quit publishing by financial pressures, and the unbound sheets were subsequently destroyed. "It did not bring Lovecraft the recognition I hoped it would bring him," lamented the publisher.

It was not until two years after Lovecraft's death that an omnibus volume of his best work was published by Arkham House (named after Lovecraft's fictional New England town), set up by young authors August Derleth and Donald Wandrei solely to preserve the collected writings of their literary mentor between hardcovers.

August William Derleth sold his first story when he was only fifteen. He began corresponding with Lovecraft in August 1926, two years after he had first read 'The Rats in the Walls' in "The Unique Magazine".

Many years later, Frank Belknap Long, Jr. observed: "One of August Derleth's most remarkable achievements was his success in gaining wide recognition as a regional novelist at an age when most young writers, even those of exceptional promise, are content with three or four favorable reviews.

"When I met him for the first time at Howard Wandrei's studio apartment just north of Greenwich Village, that early recognition was at its height, and can only be thought of as extraordinary."

Author E. Hoffman Price, who had first met Derleth in the early 1950s, recalled that: "August was overweight, but no matter how many pounds he lost, his height combined with breadth of frame would make him conspicuous.

"Square of shoulders: square face; a head of wavy dark hair—amiable eyes and ready smile which would throw the unwary off guard—August was reputed to be irritable, cantankerous, short tempered, and mule stubborn."

In a letter to Clark Ashton Smith, dated October 12, 1926 Lovecraft revealed: "I have just discovered a boy of seventeen who promises to develop into something of a fantaisiste. He is August W. Derleth, whose name you may have seen as author of some rather immature stories in *Weird Tales*. Finding my address through the magazine, he began corresponding with me; & turns out to be a veritable little prodigy; devoted to Dunsany & Arthur Machen, & ambitious to excel in their chosen field."

Totalling around some 1,000 letters, the correspondence between Lovecraft and his young protégé continued for eleven years, up until a month before the older man's untimely death.

"His rationalizations—his beliefs—his attitudes directly and subtly colored my own and helped me to take long strides toward maturity both as a writer and a man," Derleth recalled fifty years later.

Teaming up with Minneapolis correspondent Donald Wandrei (and reportedly with some additional input from fellow writer J. Vernon Shea), Derleth started work on putting together a tribute volume to Lovecraft. The result was a huge collection entitled *The Outsider and Others*, containing thirty-six stories and the influential essay 'Supernatural Horror in Literature'.

As Derleth explained in 1970, the title was chosen "because 'The Outsider' was not only a favorite Lovecraft tale, but also because Lovecraft himself was rather an outsider in his time."

However, when two New York publishers rejected the book, one of the editors suggested that Derleth and Wandrei publish it themselves. This they did, creating the Arkham House imprint. "There was never any question about the name of our publishing house," Derleth later recalled.

Utilising some of the mortgage money Derleth had borrowed from a local bank to build a house, *The Outsider and Others* was published in 1939 in an edition of 1,268 copies. The dust jacket illustration was by famed fantasy artist Virgil Finlay. Despite selling the hefty volume for just $5.00 (or $3.50 pre-publication price), Arkham House only received 150 advance orders. Derleth put an advertisement in *Weird Tales*, but the book moved slowly. It eventually took four years to sell out its only printing and recoup its original investment.

"In the beginning it took great courage, perseverance, and foresight to get Arkham House established," revealed Frank Belknap Long, "and both Derleth and Wandrei strained their modest resources to the utmost, making more than one personal sacrifice to ensure that there would be a wide and discriminating audience for HPL's first short story collection in hardcover."

To enable the small press to continue, Derleth was forced to publish collections by himself and Clark Ashton Smith to help alleviate the imprint's cash-flow problems.

"The buyers of our first book were sufficiently enthusiastic to persuade me to believe there might be a market for small editions of books in the general domain of fantasy, perhaps with emphasis on the macabre or science fiction," Derleth explained.

THE OUTSIDER AND OTHERS

BY H.P. LOVECRAFT

XVIII

"Lovecraft could hardly have guessed that he had made the friend who was in time to make him famous."

—Lin Carter

PRIOR TO HIS death, H.P. Lovecraft had named his teenage Florida correspondent Robert Hayward Barlow as his literary executor. "Other instructions concerned books to be returned or bequeathed," Barlow wrote in 1944. "Mrs. Gamwell copied out this list in longhand for me, since she wished the original as a sad memento, and her copy I still have. Had I published it then, some misunder-standings and ill-feeling which caused her and me distress, might have been avoided."

"He was no more capable of acting as Lovecraft's literary executor than of commanding an army in battle," E. Hoffman Price remembered. "Only a man as impractical and unrealistic as H.P. Lovecraft would ever have appointed him to such a position."

Lovecraft's "boy prodigy" had wanted to publish his own Lovecraft volume, but August Derleth and Donald Wandrei eventually convinced Barlow to hand over all the material to them or to Brown University Library in Providence.

In her 1997 biography, *Derleth: Hawk... and Dove*, Dorothy M. Grobe Litersky revealed that, according to Derleth, Lovecraft's aunt had "signed over any possible profits from the venture, and years later, claimed Mrs. Gamwell had willed Lovecraft's rights to them, also."

Many Lovecraft fans (as well as authors such as J. Vernon Shea) have questioned Derleth's version of events over the years, although the aunt certainly left Derleth and Wandrei all royalties, in equal shares, that were owed to her from the first Arkham House collection.

It is apparent that many of Lovecraft's early stories were in the public domain, having been originally published in uncopyrighted amateur publications. Litersky also noted in her biography of Derleth that, "In the case of Lovecraft material, like the individual stories in *The Outsider and Others*, which were in the public domain, he [Derleth] went right ahead and threatened suit anyway, knowing he didn't have a leg to stand on. Many authors who wanted permission to publish reprints of Arkham House copyrighted material, paid him more out of a feeling of moral obligation than because they thought he had a legal right to refuse that permission."

Derleth's successor at Arkham House, James Turner, maintained in 1990 that "Only a qualified attorney could speak authoritatively on the labyrinthine nature of the Lovecraft copyrights." However, Turner's own successor at the imprint, Peter Ruber, claimed a decade later that as a result of a lawsuit filed against the imprint by Donald Wandrei, Arkham's attorney had "removed a considerable amount of documentary evidence" which contained details of the acquisition of Lovecraft's literary estate.

This "evidence" apparently included correspondence from the executors of Lovecraft's aunt's estate, which assigned the publishing rights to all Lovecraft's properties to Derleth and Wandrei. In October 1947, Derleth reportedly forwarded notarised copies of these assignments to the editor of *Weird Tales*.

Whatever the true facts, there is no doubt that August Derleth's almost-obsessive protection of the Lovecraft material eventually resulted in lifting the author's reputation out of the small press and pulp arenas and into the world of mass-market literature.

As Lin Carter later observed: "In 1926, when he casually sent off a friendly reply to a fan letter from a seventeen-year-old reader in Sauk City, Wisconsin, Lovecraft could hardly have guessed that he had made the friend who was in time to make him famous."

"Without Derleth there would be no Lovecraft following today," echoed Peter Ruber. "By the same token, without Lovecraft there would be no Arkham House today. It was a rare and symbiotic relationship of the best kind."

August Derleth soon became Lovecraft's chief literary disciple, subsequently inheriting his papers and writing a number of posthumous collaborations based on notes and fragments which Lovecraft had left undeveloped. 'The Survivor' (*Weird Tales*, July 1954) was the story closest to completion at the time of the author's death, but others include 'The Lamp of Alhazred' (which features Lovecraft himself as a character), 'The Shuttered Room' and the short novel *The Lurker at the Threshold* (1945).

There is no doubt that Derleth's influence on the development of the Cthulhu Mythos (a term he himself coined—Lovecraft had never referred to his story-cycle by title) was profound. He picked up from where Lovecraft had left it, and developed it into a more coherent, although some might argue more prosaic, whole.

"Death Thumbs a Ride" by ROBERT ARTHUR

MAY

Weird Tales

20¢

A Thriller Classic

THE SHADOW OVER INNSMOUTH

by

H. P. LOVECRAFT

SEABURY QUINN   •   NELSON S. BOND

XIX

"There will never be another like him."

—Edmond Hamilton

MEANWHILE, EDITOR Farnsworth Wright had marked Lovecraft's passing in the June 1937 edition of *Weird Tales* with a personal eulogy: "Sad indeed is the news that tells us of H.P. Lovecraft's death. He was a titan of weird and fantastic literature, whose literary achievements and impeccable craftsmanship were acclaimed throughout the English-speaking world... His death is a serious loss to weird and fantastic fiction; but to the editors of *Weird Tales* the personal loss takes precedence."

The following month's issue contained the memorial poem 'To Howard Phillips Lovecraft' by Clark Ashton Smith. "I am profoundly saddened by the news of H.P. Lovecraft's death after a month of painful illness," Smith wrote in that issue's 'The Eyrie'. "The loss seems an intolerable one, and I am sure that it will be felt deeply and permanently by the whole weird fiction public. Most of all will it be felt by the myriad friends who knew Lovecraft through face-to-face meeting or correspondence; for in his case the highest literary genius was allied to the most brilliant and most endearing personal qualities."

Other tributes to the author from his contemporaries filled out the letter column in the same issue: "I just heard the news of H.P.

Lovecraft's recent death," wrote Edmond Hamilton. "This is quite a shock, coming so soon after the death of [Robert E.] Howard. While I never met either of them, I have been appearing with them in *Weird Tales* for so long that I had a dim feeling of acquaintance. I think I read every one of Lovecraft's stories from 'Dagon', years ago. It is too bad that he is gone—there will never be another like him."

"I've been feeling extremely depressed about Lovecraft's death," echoed Henry Kuttner. "Even now I can't realize it. He was my literary idol since the days of 'The Horror at Red Hook', and lately a personal friend as well. The loss to literature is a very great one, but the loss to HPL's friends is greater."

Kenneth Sterling, a young friend whose interplanetary story 'In the Walls of Eryx' Lovecraft rewrote and which would later be published under a collaborative by-line, added his own tribute: "A contributor to *Weird Tales* since its inception, he has always been considered one of the leading writers of modern weird literature and was, in my opinion, the pre-eminent creative artist in this field. His vivid, powerful style, unsurpassed in producing and sustaining a mood of horror is well known to you and your readers. His decease leaves a gap which can never be filled."

Starting with the July 1937 issue, *Weird Tales* included something by Lovecraft in seventeen successive issues. These contributions mostly consisted of reprints (sometimes from other magazines), previously rejected tales and poetry.

There were also some "new" stories which carried the Lovecraft by-line: 'The Shunned House' had initially been rejected by Wright in 1924, and Lovecraft's friends W. Paul Cook and Robert H. Barlow had both attempted to publish the tale in book form. Cook had printed approximately 300 copies with an introduction by Frank Belknap Long for The Recluse Press back in 1928. Intended to be Lovecraft's first book, no more than a dozen or so copies were reportedly bound up by Barlow in the mid-1930s, including a leather-bound copy for the author, with the remainder sold for $1.00 apiece.

"A young friend of Lovecraft's wanted very much to have the sheets," recalled Cook, "promising to bind them adequately and send the books out at once. I had my doubts; but Howard seemed to wish to give the boy a chance at the book, so I turned it over to him. That is the last I ever heard from the enterprise, and do not know the fate of the prints."

It was not until 1959 that Arkham House sold off around fifty sets of the remaining sheets in the unbound state, before binding up the remaining 100 or so copies in its possession and offering them for sale in 1961. A forged photo-offset edition of *The Shunned House* produced in the mid-1960s also exists.

'The Wicked Clergyman' (aka 'The Evil Clergyman'), a short tale originally written in 1937 as a portion of a letter and never intended for publication, appeared in the April 1939 *Weird Tales*, while Kenneth Sterling's science fiction story 'In the Walls of Eryx', extensively rewritten by Lovecraft back in January 1936, appeared under both names in the October 1939 issue.

Although at least two stories by Lovecraft—one a rewrite featuring Clark Ashton Smith's toad-god Tsathoggua and the other about a cursed Providence hotel—were both reputedly lost, other "stories" began appearing in various small press magazines. Again, these were often early fragments or extracts from letters and included 'The Book', an unfinished tale started in 1934. Of even more interest was 'Azathoth', published in the second and final issue of Robert Barlow's *Leaves* (1938). Reputedly the beginning of a never-completed novel that Lovecraft started writing in June 1922, it was the first instance of the eponymous entity being mentioned in the author's work.

Meanwhile, after 179 issues, illness and economics finally forced Farnsworth Wright to relinquish editorial control of *Weird Tales*. Although he stayed on for a brief time as editor, the March

1940 edition was his last as the debilitations of Parkinson's disease eventually took their toll. No longer able to walk without assistance, he died in June that same year as a result of an operation designed to alleviate his condition.

With editorial offices transferred from Chicago to New York, *Weird Tales* continued under the editorship of Dorothy McIlwraith, a middle-aged Scottish woman. Although she never displayed Farnsworth Wright's talent for editing, McIlwraith bought several Lovecraft stories.

Despite rejecting 'The Dream-Quest of Unknown Kadath', in June 1941 McIllwraith decided to take Lovecraft's 'The Shadow Over Innsmouth', but only if Derleth agreed to cut the 26,000-word story to 15,000 words. It appeared in severely truncated form in the January 1942 issue.

In Canada the same issue appeared in May that year, but with different cover and interior artwork due to that country's wartime import restrictions. Whereas the American edition featured an uncredited painting that had nothing to do with the contents, the Canadian variant used a distinctive depiction of Lovecraft's ichthyological "Deep Ones" by Edmond Good, thus making it the only issue of *Weird Tales* in the history of the magazine to feature an illustration for a credited H.P. Lovecraft story on its cover.

August Derleth and Donald Wandrei borrowed a typescript Derleth had prepared some years earlier of Lovecraft's 48,000-word novella 'The Case of Charles Dexter Ward' (written January–March, 1927) from Robert H. Barlow and had it professionally re-typed. The author's original hand-written manuscript had proved something of a problem, as Derleth recalled in 'The Eyrie':

"The story was written in longhand on the reverse side of letters he had received, some 130 or 140 sheets of all sizes and colors. He didn't believe in margins or "white space". Every sheet was crowded from top to bottom, from left edge to right, with his small, cramped handwriting.

"That was his original draft; you can imagine what happened when he got through revising, words and sentences crossed out or written in, whole paragraphs added, inserts put on the back of the sheet where they got tangled up with the letters from his correspondents, and the inserts rewritten with additional paragraphs to be put in the insert which was to be put in its proper place in the story.

"Lovecraft's handwriting was not easy to read under the best of circumstances; he had his own peculiarities of spelling, often used Latin and Greek phrases, and often used coined words of his own. These made the problem of deciphering his complex puzzle-pages even more difficult. All in all, working after my classes at the U., it took me four months to get through the labyrinth."

It took two months to prepare and proof a fresh typescript for the story's abridged appearance under the blurb "Last of the Lovecrafts" in the May and July 1941 issues of *Weird Tales*. The unexpurgated version was eventually published in Arkham's second bumper collection of Lovecraft stories, *Beyond the Wall of Sleep* (1943).

LOST WORLDS

CLARK ASHTON SMITH

XX

"His sculptures, which are especially powerful and fascinating, are cut largely from strange and unusual minerals and have been compared to pre-Columbian art."
—August Derleth

FOLLOWING LOVECRAFT'S UNTIMELY death, Clark Ashton Smith's enthusiasm for fiction appears to have waned. The criticisms of editors had taken their toll, and many of those tales Smith considered his finest had initially been rejected or revised. His aged parents had become more dependent on him over the years, and alongside the nursing duties he found himself doing all the household chores as well.

He also apparently had a recurrence of the nervous disorder which had reduced him to a near-invalid for eight years in 1913, developing a "nerve-fatigue or exhaustion" which prevented him from writing and apparently left him feeling bitter and resentful. He also especially hated living in Auburn.

Smith's mother had died in September 1935 and his father, who had suffered from high blood pressure and a weak heart, followed two years later, the day after Christmas. Smith was forced to sell all but two acres of the family property to pay for the funeral expenses.

In a 1937 letter to illustrator Virgil Finlay he admitted: "As for my writing, circumstances have made me very unproductive during the past two years. My mother's illness and death, my father's growing feebleness, and our virtual isolation with everything devolving around me, are chiefly responsible for my lapse from the pages of W.T."

Weird Tales, which had published most of Smith's stories, only paid a cent a word, and the author was forced to use a lawyer to obtain his payment due from *Wonder Stories*. As a consequence he had to live frugally, and between 1941 and 1945, Smith performed "monotonous and irksome" part-time ranch and orchard work to supplement his meagre income.

In September 1937, he revealed to Finlay that the sale of several small carvings and a pseudo-science short story to *Thrilling Wonder Stories* had resulted in a monthly income of $65.50. "If such sales continue, I shall become a bloated plutocrat!" he joked. "Anyway, I won't need to dig so often or so deeply in the old boneyard."

However, decline in the family finances resulted in Smith taking a number of menial jobs such as well-digger, fruit-picker and packer, wood-chopper, typist, cement-mixer, gardener, hard-rock miner, mucker and windlasser, to support himself.

"Though his verse may occasionally sound as if Smith lived in an ivory tower," explained August Derleth, "this is far indeed from the facts."

Around 1937, Smith had submitted a selection of his poems to a British publisher, but nothing came of it. However, he had already made his first British hardcover appearance four years earlier, with 'Isle of the Torturers' in *Keep on the Light*, the ninth volume in the "Not at Night" anthology series edited by Christine Campbell Thomson. Smith also contributed to eight issues of the British pulp magazine *Tales of Wonder* between 1939 and 1942, and he had a pair of stories reprinted in the only two issues of the British booklet *Strange Tales* (1946). One of these was 'The Nameless Offspring', written in 1931 and which (like 'The Gorgon', completed the year before) is set in contemporary England. Inspired by Arthur Machen's 'The Great God Pan', the author described it as being "about as diabolic as anything I am ever likely to devise".

Smith developed an alcohol problem in the late 1930s and early '40s, although liquor had no perceptible effect on him. E. Hoffman Price once recalled watching him drink three or four tumblers of 151-proof Demerara rum, three fingers deep. All that happened was "the deep-lined melancholy of his old, old face brightened slightly, and a new twinkle came into his eyes".

While Smith had virtually abandoned his fiction writing during this period, he continued composing poetry and working on various artistic projects.

Then in 1942, Smith's first major collection of fiction appeared from Arkham House, the small press imprint established in 1939 by August Derleth and Donald Wandrei to preserve their friend Lovecraft's fiction between durable hardcovers.

Selected by the author himself, *Out of Space and Time* was only the third offering from the new imprint, and because neither Derleth nor Smith seriously expected that Arkham House would survive long enough to issue a second collection by the author, Smith included twenty of what he considered his favourite and best fantasy and horror stories published up to that time. With a dust jacket illustration by *Weird Tales* artist Hannes Bok, the book was limited to just 1,054 copies.

However, mostly due to Derleth's tenacity, Arkham House did barely continue. Several of Smith's unique rock carvings were photographed for the dust jacket of the second Lovecraft omnibus, *Beyond the Wall of Sleep* (1943), and the following year the imprint also issued a second collection of Smith's own fiction, *Lost Worlds*, with the contents again selected by the author. This time 2,043 copies were printed and the dust jacket was illustrated with a photograph of four of Smith's creations.

Smith's sculptures were often carved outside with a small

pocketknife from soapstone, talc and a white chalky material he found locally and called "diatomite". The carvings, which often had such evocative titles as 'The Outsider', 'Cthulhu', 'Inquisitor Morghi', 'Wizard Eibon' and 'Spawn of Cthulhu', were then finished with sandpaper and "fired" in the kitchen stove to harden them.

"His sculptures, which are especially powerful and fascinating, are cut largely from strange and unusual minerals and have been compared to pre-Columbian art," revealed Derleth, who himself managed to assemble a personal collection of nearly fifty carvings by Smith.

The first issue of *The Arkham Sampler* (Winter, 1948) included an extensive checklist of titles and descriptions of sculptures, probably compiled by Smith himself. However, while more carvings were listed in a letter in a later edition, Arkham House's previously-announced volume entitled *Sculptures by Clark Ashton Smith* (aka *Cthulhu and Others in Stone*), like so many of that precarious imprint's forthcoming projects, remained unpublished.

According to writer Edmond Hamilton, while visiting Smith in Auburn he noticed that some of the stones lying around the author's cabin had faces and other weird effigies carved on them. Apparently, when Smith did not like a sculpture he was working on, he would simply throw it out of the window onto the gravel surrounding his home.

CLARK ASHTON SMITH

AVON

Fantasy

READER No. 12

35¢

THE BLONDE GODDESS OF BAL-SAGOTH by Robert E. Howard

also stories by
Sax Rohmer
Miles J. Breuer
Clark Ashton Smith
AND OTHERS

XXI

"I would say Lovecraft's work must stand or fall by
virtue of those stories he completed himself, presented
for publication, and had accepted for publication."

—Robert Bloch

AFTER DONALD WANDREI joined the US Army in 1942
and was sent to Europe, he left the day-to-day running of
Arkham House to August Derleth, except for editing Lovecraft's
voluminous body of letters for future publication. Derleth was
considered physically unfit for service because of his high blood
pressure.

Given his popularity in *Weird Tales* and other magazines, it is
perhaps surprising that Arkham House did not get around to
publishing the first major collection of Robert E. Howard's fiction
until 1946. But when it did, August Derleth made sure that *Skull-
Face and Others* was something special. Issued as an oversized
hardcover (a format which the publisher only used for prestige
volumes) and boasting a full-colour cover painting by Hannes Bok,
the book contained a generous twenty-three stories along with a
scattering of non-fiction pieces.

As August Derleth revealed in his Foreword, "Though the
present volume of his work is primarily a selection of those of his
stories which appeared in *Weird Tales*, I have striven to make it as
representative as possible of his best work."

Derleth went on to defend his choice: "Quite possibly all his best stories are not included in this collection. I re-read everything from *Weird Tales* and *Strange Tales*, and in my considered judgement the stories here collected represent the best work he did. In matters of taste, however, there is no argument; though others may think differently."

He also revealed that he did not feel justified including more of Howard's Conan adventures, although he managed to find room for 'The Phoenix on the Sword', 'The Scarlet Citadel', 'The Tower of the Elephant', 'Rogues in the House' and 'Shadows in Zamboula'.

Unfortunately—perhaps due to the volume's higher $5.00 price tag—the 3,037 print-run sold slowly, and it would be another seventeen years until Arkham followed it up with a collection of Howard's "secondary" stories, *The Dark Man and Others* (1963). In the meantime, Glenn Lord collected all of Howard's known verse at the time into the slender Arkham volume *Always Comes Evening: The Collected Poems of Robert E. Howard* (1957), which he also paid to have published in a small printing of 636 copies. Even so, it still took eight years for the title to go out-of-print.

According to August Derleth, he contributed $25,000 from his own income as a writer to keep Arkham House running over the imprint's first ten years. Consequently, once paper rationing was over, he began publishing more books by contemporaries of his and Lovecraft's.

Signing up some of the foremost fantasy and horror authors on both sides of the Atlantic, Arkham produced volumes by not only Robert E. Howard and Clark Ashton Smith, but also Henry S. Whitehead, A.E. Coppard, Robert Bloch, J. Sheridan Le Fanu, Frank Belknap Long, Algernon Blackwood, William Hope Hodgson, H. Russell Wakefield, Lady Cynthia Asquith, Ray Bradbury, Carl Jacobi, Fritz Leiber Jr., L.P. Hartley, Lord Dunsany and Seabury Quinn, along with titles by Derleth and Wandrei themselves.

Publication of these and other authors allowed Derleth to keep the Arkham House imprint in the public eye while he prepared more collections of Lovecraft's work, many of which contained lesser material along with revisions or collaborations. These later Lovecraft volumes included such titles as *Marginalia* (1944), *Something About Cats and Other Pieces* (1949), *The Survivor and Others* (1957), *The Shuttered Room and Other Pieces* (1959), *Dreams and Fancies* (1962), *Collected Poems* (1963) and *The Dark Brotherhood and Other Pieces* (1966).

"I would say Lovecraft's work must stand or fall by virtue of those stories he completed himself, presented for publication, and had accepted for publication," stated Robert Bloch in the 1960s. "I agree in part that perhaps a greater share of the material would not have been approved by Lovecraft himself."

Apparently sponsored by Arkham House, *Best Supernatural Stories of H.P. Lovecraft*, edited with an introduction by Derleth, appeared as a mass-market hardcover from The World Publishing Company in 1945. The first "popular-priced edition" of the author's work, it went through three printings in just over a year.

The Weird Shadow Over Innsmouth and Other Stories of the Supernatural (1944) and *The Dunwich Horror* (1945) appeared in early paperback editions from Bartholomew House. They were followed by *The Dunwich Horror and Other Weird Tales* (1945) in a special Armed Services Edition. In 1947, the Avon Book Company published a pocket edition of *The Lurking Fear and Other Pieces* (reprinted eleven years later as *Cry Horror!*).

In 1945, New York publisher Ben Abramson issued Lovecraft's essay *Supernatural Horror in Literature* in a separate hardcover printing, with a new foreword by August Derleth. The essay has since been republished in various editions, including a softcover from Dover Publications in 1973 (with an introduction by E.F. Bleiler) and as an illustrated edition from Montilla Publications in 1992.

Despite being rejected by *Weird Tales*, Lovecraft's 'The Dream-Quest of Unknown Kadath' had eventually appeared in *Beyond the Wall of Sleep*. As Derleth explained in his introduction when the story was subsequently serialised over the first four issues of *The Arkham Sampler* (1948): "It seems clearly evident that, had he lived longer, Lovecraft would have spent more time on a revision of this novel, which was left in first draft and, in the large part, not typewritten." In 1956, Shroud Publishers of Buffalo, New York, produced a separate 1,500-copy paperbound edition along with a small-run hardcover printing that sold for $10.00 apiece.

Meanwhile, Robert E. Howard's tragic death did not mark the end of Conan either. The unpublished manuscripts of four completed Conan stories, which had been rejected by *Weird Tales* editor Farnsworth Wright, were discovered amongst the author's papers many years after his death.

The first of these, 'The God in the Bowl', appeared in the September 1952 issue of *Space Science Fiction*. A combination of murder mystery and magic, it was revised considerably for publication by writer L. Sprague de Camp, who produced yet another version of the story, closer to the original manuscript, for paperback publication fifteen years later.

Another greatly abridged version by de Camp of Howard's story 'The Black Stranger' appeared in the first issue of *Fantasy Magazine* for February–March, 1953. "It was quite an event to discover that a full novelette by [Howard] had never been published," wrote editor Lester Del Rey, "and we finally got it. It isn't the sort of a tale you'll usually find in this magazine—because nobody else can quite recapture the pre-mythical past."

This 33,000-word short novel had been written around the same time as 'Beyond the Black River' and 'Wolves Beyond the Border' and mixed Conan with Picts and pirates. When he could not sell it as a Conan adventure, Howard had attempted to rescue the story by turning the hero into swashbuckling pirate Black

Vulmea, but that version remained unpublished until 1976, when it appeared in the collection *Black Vulmea's Vengeance* under the title 'Swords of the Red Brotherhood'. The Conan treatment was subsequently republished under the title 'The Treasure of Tranicos', and the complete version finally saw print, exactly as Howard wrote it, in Karl Edward Wagner's 1987 anthology *Echoes of Valor*.

Originally rejected by Wright in 1932, Howard had submitted a revised draft of 'The Frost King's Daughter', featuring the Conan-like hero Amra of Akbitana, to the amateur journal *The Fantasy Fan*, which had published the story in the March 1934 issue as 'Gods of the North'. When Howard's Conan version appeared in the August 1953 issue of *Fantasy Fiction* as 'The Frost-Giant's Daughter', it had been extensively rewritten by de Camp, and it was not until 1976 that the author's original manuscript finally saw print.

Although *Fantasy Fiction* had claimed, "Here, for the last time in an original story, the barbarian hero stalks through the strange, magic-ridden lands of the Hyperborean [*sic*] Age", another Conan story, 'The Vale of Lost Women', eventually appeared in the Spring 1967 issue of Robert A.W. Lowndes' *Magazine of Horror*.

This story was most probably rejected by Farnsworth Wright because of scenes in which an older Conan massacred an entire village, and the heroine had to barter her virginity in order to be rescued. Reaction to its publication was decidedly mixed: "The so-called 'Conan' story with its fantasy domino slightly askew is a thinly-masked 'porny' of the cheapest sado-sexual variety and doesn't belong in your pages," wrote one reader to the magazine's letters column, while another was of the opinion: "I cannot imagine why 'The Vale of Lost Women' was not published during Howard's lifetime... It is certainly one of Howard's better works."

Robert E. Howard also left behind a number of fragments and brief outlines for never-completed adventures which various authors, including L. Sprague de Camp and Lin Carter, completed and added to in an attempt to fill in the gaps in Conan's career in much the same manner that August Derleth and others expanded upon Lovecraft's Cthulhu Mythos. Some of these Howard manuscripts were Oriental adventures that the writers then converted into Conan stories by changing names, deleting anachronisms and introducing a supernatural element.

In 1953, Ace Books issued Howard's novel *Conan the Conqueror* as an "Ace Double" paperback, bound back-to-back with *The Sword of Rhiannon* by Leigh Brackett, and the following year the book finally made its British debut, exactly twenty years after it had first been submitted by Howard, in a hardcover edition from T.V. Boardman & Company of London. Unfortunately, the uncredited dust jacket artist decided to illustrate the same scene that Margaret Brundage had used for her cover of the December 1935 *Weird Tales*, with equally wretched results.

Between 1950–57 New York's Gnome Press published seven hardcover volumes of Conan stories: *Conan the Conqueror, The Sword of Conan, King Conan, The Coming of Conan, Conan the Barbarian, Tales of Conan* and *The Return of Conan*. These included several tales either edited by or in collaboration with de Camp, who later explained: "Late in 1951, I stumbled upon a cache of Howard's manuscripts in the apartment of the then literary agent for Howard's estate... The incomplete state of the Conan saga has tempted me and others to add to it, as Howard might have done had he lived... The reader must judge how successful our posthumous collaboration with Howard has been."

However, author and editor Karl Edward Wagner appeared to echo Robert Bloch's opinions about Lovecraft imitations when, in 1977, he wrote: "The only man who could write a Robert E. Howard story was Robert E. Howard. It is far more than a matter of imitating adjective usage or analyzing comma-splices. It is a matter of spirit. Pastiche-Conan is not the same Conan as portrayed by Robert E. Howard. Read such, as it pleases you—but don't delude yourself into thinking that this is any more Robert E.

Howard's Conan than a Conan story you decided to write yourself. It is this editor's belief that a Conan collection should contain *only* Robert E. Howard's Conan tales, and that *no* editorial emendations should alter the authenticity of Howard's creation." And this coming from one of the better writers of Howard pastiches.

In fact, *Weird Tales* editor Farnsworth Wright had told his readers much the same thing four decades earlier: "Sorry to deny your request for some other author to carry on the Conan stories of the late Robert E. Howard. His work was touched with genius, and he had a distinctive style of writing that put the stamp of his personality on every story he wrote. It would hardly be fair to his memory if we allowed Conan to be recreated by another hand, no matter how skillful."

A mixture of fantasy and historical adventure featuring the 11th century Irishman Turlogh O'Brien, 'The Gods of Bal-Sagoth'—which had originally appeared in *Weird Tales* in 1931—was reprinted in 1950 in the twelfth volume of Donald A. Wollheim's *Avon Fantasy Reader* under the slightly sexed-up title 'The Blonde Goddess of Bal-Sagoth', with an appropriately cheesecake cover illustration by Filipino artist Manuel Rey Isip.

"During his unfortunately brief lifetime," recalled Wollheim in his introduction to the story, "Robert E. Howard was as prolific a writer as anyone might hope for. He was that sort of natural writer to whom the speed of narrating a tale did not interfere with the quality.

"He *liked* to write—and that is the secret of most good fiction. And he loved nothing better than a lusty, gusty tale of uninhibited men battling fiercely against a primitive environment. Add to that the fulsome colour of the mystery and magic of the past: the horizons clouded with mist and fearsome legendry, the heavens a conspiracy of supernatural powers, and fellow men nearly as dangerous and unpredictable as the beasts of the field, and a Robert E. Howard story is bound to be an epic of weird and exciting peril."

XXII

"A very fine poet who never received the recognition
he deserved and whose entire life was, in the main,
ill-starred, made somber by the frustration which
one could sense in almost everything he wrote."
—Frank Belknap Long

THROUGHOUT THE 1940s and early '50s Clark Ashton
Smith was visited in Auburn by fellow writers such as Henry
Kuttner, E. Hoffman Price, Jack Williamson, Donald Wandrei
(who had first visited the author in 1934), R.H. Barlow, Henry
Hasse, Emil Petaja, Fritz Leiber and August Derleth.

Smith's third Arkham House volume, *Genius Loci and Other
Tales* (1948), contained sixteen stories mostly selected from *Weird
Tales*. It appeared in an edition of 3,047 copies and remained in
print for many years, resulting in Derleth reducing the print run of
his next Smith collection, not published until twelve years later.

The Ghoul and the Seraph (1950) was a slim booklet totalling
eighty-five copies issued by Michael deAngelis' short-lived
Gargoyle Press of Brooklyn. It reprinted Smith's short play from
Ebony and Crystal in its first separate publication.

Despite copies of *Odes and Sonnets* being remaindered in the
mid-1940s for just $1.00 each, Smith had started compiling a large
collection of his verse. In December 1949, he had submitted a
manuscript of more than 500 poems to Arkham House for a
volume to be called *The Hashish-Eater and Other Poems*. Although

the title was periodically announced as forthcoming, Derleth was concerned that the cover price would be prohibitive and that sales would not recoup the book's production costs. As a result, Derleth compromised by issuing *The Dark Château* in 1951 as a slim limited edition hardcover of only 563 copies.

"Lovers of good poetry will turn to Smith's verse with lasting delight," proclaimed the dust wrapper blurb. "Eschewing obscurity, scorning incoherence, Clark Ashton Smith writes of the mystical and strange, of the worlds of the mind and the heart so near and yet so far from so many people in our time."

Derleth had been right to be cautious. Even with its low print run, *The Dark Château* did not sell out until nine years later at a list price of $2.50. However, that did not prevent him from publishing a second selection of Smith's verse in 1958. The dust jacket blurb for *Spells and Philtres* promised the reader that the contents would "enchant and delight the lover of poetry and the macabre, for they are new ventures into the mystical half-world which beckons forever at the edge of awareness."

At least Derleth was finally learning some business acumen— *Spells and Philtres* contained fewer pages, had a smaller print run (519 copies) and cost fifty cents more than its predecessor.

Donald Wandrei, who "had the great pleasure" of proofing the book's galleys, wrote to Smith in 1957 and reassured the author that "August and I of course hope to see your big Selected (or Collected) Poems become a realized project." Regrettably, Smith would not live to see the volume published.

By now Smith was in his early sixties. As George F. Haas recalled, after meeting him in 1953: "He was slightly stooped but, I should judge, about five feet, eleven inches in height. He wore a short moustache. His hair was light brown, straight, and although I looked later, I could not detect a single grey hair. His wide, high-domed forehead was quite wrinkled. He seemed somewhat frail but he had an amazing barrel chest". Haas also noted that "on his head, to keep his fine silky hair from flying, was what was almost a trademark with him—a bright red beret".

On November 14, 1954, a year after suffering a heart attack, Smith entered into a late-life marriage with journalist Carolyn Jones Dorman, who had three teenage children from a previous union.

After the wedding, the couple moved from Auburn to take up semi-permanent residence at Carol's house in nearby Pacific Grove. It was some time before they moved all Smith's possessions out of the old cabin, and vandals broke in. They emptied his boxes of papers all over the floors, scattered his library of books and, in an act of desecration that affected Smith very deeply, overturned the two urns containing the ashes of his mother and father.

Even before this, rifle bullets had been fired through the walls of the empty cabin, and in 1957 the final act of vandalism occurred when the building was destroyed by fire (possibly in an attempt to convince Smith to sell the land to a real estate speculator).

To help earn a living, for a time Smith became a professional gardener in Pacific Grove. However, he was not physically suited to the work and he hated it. He much preferred the wild flowers of the Sierran foothills.

However, perhaps because of his marriage, Smith experienced another burst of creative energy during the middle to late 1950s, when he produced his final batch of new short fiction.

Rising production costs and reduced sales resulted in Derleth publishing Smith's fourth Arkham House collection, *The Abominations of Yondo* (1960), in an edition of just over 2,000 copies. It once again featured a cover photograph of the author's weird sculptures.

It would be his final book published during his lifetime. Suffering from ill-health after a series of minor strokes, Clark Ashton Smith died peacefully in his sleep in Pacific Grove on August 14, 1961. He was aged sixty-eight.

His last story was 'The Dart of Rasasfa', completed in July 1961, just three weeks before the author's death. Although the tale had been commissioned around a George Barr cover for an upcoming issue of *Fantastic Stories of Imagination*, the editor ultimately rejected it.

In a letter to August Derleth written that same August, Frank Belknap Long described Smith as "a very fine poet who never received the recognition he deserved and whose entire life was, in the main, ill-starred, made somber by the frustration which one could sense in almost everything he wrote".

After Smith's death, his widow married Frank Wakefield, a West Coast artist who illustrated several Arkham House dust jackets during the 1940s, including Smith's own *Genius Loci and Other Tales*. Wakefield was an alcoholic, and Carol eventually divorced him. She herself died of cancer in January 1973.

H.P. LOVECRAFT

3

TALES

OF

HORROR

illustrated by

Lee Brown Coye

XXIII

"August Derleth and his good friend, Donald Wandrei,
fought like tigers, year after year, to build up a
Lovecraft awareness."

—E. Hoffman Price

ROY A. SQUIRES, who was at one time the author's literary executor, had been working on an edition of a cycle of poems Clark Ashton Smith had written around 1939–46. With Clyde Beck, Squires published *The Hill of Dionysus*: A Selection in 1962 in three variant editions eventually totalling around 390 copies. Two poems from the collection were also issued as extremely limited booklets.

The following year Squires released seventy-two copies of *Cycles*, which was "almost certainly" Smith's last poem. *¿Dónde Duermes, Eldorado? y Otros Poemas* (1964) was a small volume of poems composed by Smith in Spanish, limited to 176 copies, and Squires also published *Nero: An Early Poem* (1964) in an edition of 381 copies.

In 1963, Mirage Press had issued *In Memorium: Clark Ashton Smith*. Edited by Jack L. Chalker, it contained reminiscences from a number of the author's friends and colleagues, along with the first publication of Smith's play 'The Dead Will Cuckold You'.

The collection *Tales of Science and Sorcery* had been assembled for publication before Smith's death, and it was published in 1964 by Arkham House in an edition of just under 2,500 copies. It included four of the author's science fiction stories, which had originally appeared in such Hugo Gernsback magazines as *Wonder Stories* and *Amazing Detective Tales*.

An extended prose-poem by Smith written in 1929, 'Told in the Desert' appeared in *Over the Edge: New Stories of the Macabre* (1964), editor August Derleth's anthology marking the 25th anniversary of Arkham House. The volume contained eighteen original stories, including "a final, unpublished adventure of Solomon Kane" by Robert E. Howard—'The Blue Flame of Vengeance'—which was revised and completed by young Kansas City writer John Pocsik, who also had his first story published in the same book.

"In the tales concerning Solomon Kane, Bran Mak Morn, King Kull, and Conan," wrote Derleth, "there is quite possibly more blood-letting and more lusty carnage than in any other group of stories which appeared in pulp magazines in America during the 1930s."

H.P. Lovecraft was also included in the book with 'The Shadow in the Attic', one of a number of "posthumous collaborations" with August Derleth.

Beginning with *The Dunwich Horror and Others* in 1963 (basically *The Best Supernatural Stories of H.P. Lovecraft* with two extra tales and a new introduction), Arkham House began publishing definitive collections of Lovecraft's fiction which have been kept in print ever since. Two further volumes, *At the Mountains of Madness and Other Novels* and *Dagon and Other Macabre Tales*, appeared in 1964 and 1965, respectively.

"August Derleth and his good friend, Donald Wandrei, fought like tigers, year after year, to build up a Lovecraft awareness," explained E. Hoffman Price, "and in so doing, contributed to giving momentum to what became, finally, a fantasy boom."

"It is a testament to the power of his personality that Lovecraft could elicit such devotion," observed S.T. Joshi, "even from those who had never met him but were linked only by correspondence. August Derleth and Donald Wandrei expended their own time and resources in founding a publishing company, Arkham House, initially for the sole purpose of preserving Lovecraft's work in hardcover; but Derleth never met him and Wandrei met him only fleetingly in Lovecraft's native Providence, Rhode Island, and on Lovecraft's rare visits to New York in the 1930s."

In the 1980s, Lovecraft scholar Joshi returned to the author's original hand-written and annotated manuscripts for reprints of the three "definitive" Arkham collections in "corrected" editions which ignored previous editorial changes made by August Derleth, Farnsworth Wright and others over the years. These new texts formed the basis for three volumes of Lovecraft's work published by Penguin Books as part of its "Twentieth-Century Classics" series, and Joshi also utilised Lovecraft's original texts for the Arkham House editions of *The Horror in the Museum* (1987) and *Miscellaneous Writings* (1995).

In 1948, August Derleth planned to produce a two-volume collection of Lovecraft stories illustrated by four different artists and limited to 5,000 copies. Although nothing eventually came of the idea, *3 Tales of Horror* (1967) appeared from Arkham as an oversized "prestige" hardcover. Containing 'The Colour Out of Space', 'The Dunwich Horror' and 'The Thing on the Doorstep', it boasted fifteen illustrations by East Coast regional artist Lee Brown Coye printed on coated stock.

From 1937 until 1942, Wandrei and Derleth contacted as many of Lovecraft's correspondents as they could and transcribed thousands of letters, the longest of which consisted of seventy or eighty pages. The eventual result of this enormous effort was five volumes of *Selected Letters*, published between 1965–76 (the final two books were compiled by Derleth and his successor at Arkham House, James Turner). Since then, other publishers have issued their own volumes of Lovecraft's voluminous correspondence.

"Here at Arkham House we would be the first to admit that Lovecraft would certainly not have wanted a good deal of what he wrote put into print," Derleth revealed in the mid-1960s, "and this includes not only his juvenilia, but also some of the stories praised by his readers, and his correspondence.

"Of his earliest stories he saved only 'The Beast in the Cave', 'The Transition of Juan Romero' and 'The Alchemist' as of more merit than those pieces he destroyed. Such earlier pieces as were reprinted were found in the possession of a collector, in manuscript form. Their printing by Arkham House was in limited edition only, with no reprint in any form, specifically for collectors."

What Derleth could not possibly have foreseen was that that situation was about to change, as Lovecraft's reputation and growing popularity—along with that of his friends and colleagues Robert E. Howard and Clark Ashton Smith—would soon bring them all to the attention of a new generation of fans and an increasing number of mass-market imprints.

 PANTHER BOOKS   2'6

THE CASE OF CHARLES DEXTER WARD

H. P. LOVECRAFT

□ □ □ □ FROM THE PITS
OF UNSPEAKABLE HORROR
CAME THE EVIL OF ANOTHER
TIME TO DEVOUR HIS SOUL

XXIV

"Some of Lovecraft's admirers have become Derleth
haters because of the alleged, and perhaps actual
creation of a Cthulhu Mythos by August."
　　　　　　　　　　　　　　　—E. Hoffman Price

P UBLISHED IN 1945 under both H.P. Lovecraft and August
Derleth's bylines, *The Lurker at the Threshold* was a short
novel based upon a fragment, 'The Round Tower', and unrelated
notes discovered in Lovecraft's papers totalling approximately
1,200 words. "I constructed and wrote *The Lurker at the Threshold*,
which had nowhere been laid out, planned, or plotted by
Lovecraft," explained Derleth. The book was reprinted in
Argentina in 1946 by Editorial Molino and in Britain in 1948 by
Museum Press.

After publishing no titles for three years, Arkham House
issued *The Survivor and Others* in 1957. It contained seven of the
"posthumous collaborations" between Derleth and Lovecraft,
including a variation on 'The Shadow Out of Time' entitled 'The
Shadow Out of Space', which was based on the same story notes.

August Derleth's own contributions to the Cthulhu Mythos
had been appearing in magazines since 1932. 'The Lair of the Star-
Spawn', a collaboration with Mark Schorer, was published in the
August issue of that year's *Weird Tales*.

'The Return of Hastur' was the first of the author's series of

Lovecraft pastiches. Written in 1936, it was voted the best story to appear in the March 1939 issue of *Weird Tales*. Derleth claimed that Lovecraft "saw its opening pages and the outline of my proposed development, and in consequence made several suggestions which were enthusiastically incorporated into the story."

It was one of six stories collected in the Arkham House volume *The Mask of Cthulhu* (1958), and Derleth followed it four years later with the "fix-up" novel *The Trail of Cthulhu* (1962), based around five of his stories previously published in *Weird Tales* during the 1940s and '50s.

"Derleth's Mythos tales and posthumous collaborations helped to sustain interest in Lovecraft's writing at a time when his work had little recognition," explained editor and critic Stefan Dziemianowicz, "and created a simple template for the Lovecraft pastiche that scores of later writers would use when writing stories set in Lovecraft's universe."

Although there had already been mass-market hardcover and paperback editions of Lovecraft's work dating back to the mid-1940s, and Arkham House had done its best to keep his name alive with its limited editions—at least amongst a specialist group of aficionados—the author received a surprising resurgence in popularity in the late 1960s, when a whole new generation of American college kids turned on by J.R.R. Tolkien's *The Hobbit* and *The Lord of the Rings* started looking around for equally imaginative and mind-blowing fantasy literature.

They soon discovered H.P. Lovecraft's cosmic horror stories.

Although in Britain Lovecraft had been kept in print throughout the 1950s and '60s in hardcover by Victor Gollancz and paperback by Panther Books, when in 1969 Lancer Books reissued its abridged softcover editions of *The Dunwich Horror and Others* and *The Colour Out of Space and Others* in America the floodgates quickly opened.

The following year, Ballantine's Beagle Books imprint issued the collection *The Tomb and Other Tales*, and in 1971 followed it up with *At the Mountains of Madness and Other Tales of Terror*, *The Lurking Fear and Other Stories*, *Nine Stories from The Horror in the Museum and Other Revisions* (it actually contained ten stories) and *The Shuttered Room and Other Tales of Terror* (collaborations with August Derleth).

That same year, Scholastic brought out *The Shadow Over Innsmouth and Other Stories of Horror*, while *The Dream-Quest of Unknown Kadath* appeared as the fifteenth title in Ballantine Books' prestigious "Adult Fantasy" series edited by Lin Carter. He followed it up with *The Doom That Came to Sarnath* as the twenty-sixth volume, while *Fungi from Yuggoth & Other Poems*, also from Ballantine, contained Lovecraft's acclaimed cycle of verse illustrated by Frank Utpatel.

All these books were "published by arrangement with Arkham House" and were finally a validation of August Derleth and Donald Wandrei's decision to preserve the writings of their literary mentor between hardcovers back in 1939.

Although he had done more than anyone else—often at great personal cost to himself—to keep Lovecraft's memory and work alive in the public consciousness, there is no doubt that August Derleth made extensive changes and revisions to Lovecraft's Cthulhu Mythos, which are still being dissected and criticised by fans today.

"Some of Lovecraft's admirers have become Derleth haters because of the alleged, and perhaps actual creation of a Cthulhu Mythos by August, who is said to have gone too far in imputing this 'mythos' to Lovecraft," E. Hoffman Price presciently observed.

Following gall bladder surgery from which he never fully recovered, August Derleth died unexpectedly on July 4, 1971. He was just sixty-two years old. The posthumous collection *The Watchers Out of Time and Others* (1974) was an omnibus volume of mostly previously published "collaborations" between Derleth and Lovecraft. It included the short novel *The Lurker at the Threshold* and the incomplete title story, which Derleth had been working on at the time of his death.

Despite the passing of perhaps his greatest champion, H.P. Lovecraft's reputation was now firmly established throughout the world as the 20th century's pre-eminent author of supernatural fiction.

"Oh, oh, great Gawd . . . that . . . that."

LANCER BOOKS 73-650 60¢

KING KULL

ROBERT E. HOWARD and **LIN CARTER**

A MIGHTY HERO OF WEIRD FANTASY AND
HIGH ADVENTURE BY THE CREATOR OF **CONAN**

3/6

XXV

"Find some dope who does not know that nobody but
Robert E. Howard could write a Robert E. Howard
story!"

—E. Hoffman Price

J UST AS LOVECRAFT'S horror fiction was rediscovered by a
new generation of readers in the late 1960s, so the same was
true of Robert E. Howard and his barbarian hero Conan, both of
whom came to epitomise the emerging genre of "sword & sorcery"
or "heroic fantasy".

Amateur publications such as Glenn Lord's *The Howard
Collector*, George H. Scithers' *Amra* and The Robert E. Howard
United Press Association (REHupa) rekindled interest in Howard's
fiction during the 1960s and '70s. Beginning in 1966, Lancer Books
in America—and later Sphere Books in Britain—collected the
Conan stories into a series of twelve paperbacks, many of which
featured distinctive cover paintings by Frank Frazetta.

Edited by L. Sprague de Camp, once again Howard's original
texts were altered, and the series included revisions, posthumous
collaborations, "fix-up" novels and totally new pastiches. Over a
million copies of the Lancer editions were sold during the first few
years of publication, ranking Howard second only to J.R.R. Tolkien
in the field of fantasy fiction.

Around 1955, Gnome Press had announced a collection of Howard's work entitled *The Legacy of Conan*. Although that book never appeared, according to the Administrator to the Howard Estate, Glenn Lord, it would probably have included 'Kings of the Night', 'Worms of the Earth', 'The Valley of the Worm', 'The Garden of Fear', 'The Dark Man' and 'The Gods of Bal-Sagoth'.

When asked to finish the final two chapters of a Crusader novelette which the author had left uncompleted at the time of his death, E. Hoffman Price responded, "Do you think I am *crazy*? Find some dope who does not know that nobody but Robert E. Howard could write a Robert E. Howard story!"

However, in 1957 a Swedish fan named Björn Nyberg had collaborated with L. Sprague de Camp on a new novel entitled *The Return of Conan*, and with Howard's renewed popularity, soon other authors were adding original novels to the Conan canon. These included Karl Edward Wagner, Poul Anderson, Andrew J. Offutt, Robert Jordan, John Maddox Roberts, Steve Perry, Roland Green, Leonard Carpenter and John C. Hocking.

Thirty-five years after his creator's death, Howard's mighty Cimmerian had turned into a money-spinning franchise. And it was not long before publishers started looking around for some of the author's other work which they could republish to cash-in on his renewed popularity.

In 1967, at the height of the Conan revival, Lancer Books published *King Kull* in paperback. It not only contained 'The Shadow Kingdom', 'The Mirrors of Tuzun Thune' and 'The King and the Oak', but it also included ten other stories discovered amongst Howard's papers, four of which were completed or edited by Lin Carter.

The following year, Glenn Lord collected most of the known Solomon Kane stories—including several previously unpublished pieces—in *Red Shadows*, issued as a limited edition hardcover by Donald M. Grant with illustrations by Jeff Jones. For this volume,

'The Blue Flame of Vengeance' was retitled 'Blades of the Brotherhood' and John Pocsik's posthumous additions to the story were dropped.

In the late 1970s, Bantam Books split the book into two paperback volumes, *Solomon Kane #1: Skulls in the Stars* and *Solomon Kane #2: The Hills of the Dead*. The publisher chose British horror writer Ramsey Campbell to complete the unfinished fragments 'The Castle of the Devil', 'Hawk of Basti' and 'The Children of Asshur'.

In 1969, Dell Publishing issued the paperback *Bran Mak Morn*, which not only collected the stories that had originally appeared in *Weird Tales*, but also several previously unpublished tales and poems again assembled by Glenn Lord. Frank Frazetta provided the memorable cover painting.

Noted fantasy author, editor and Robert E. Howard scholar Karl Edward Wagner—who also died tragically prematurely—was commissioned by Zebra Books to write a novel featuring Bran Mak Morn. *Legion from the Shadows* appeared in paperback in 1976.

Unfortunately, a second volume in the series by Wagner, *Queen of the Night*, was apparently never written. However, David C. Smith and Richard L. Tierney collaborated on *For the Witch of the Mists*, another original Bran Mak Morn novel that was published by Zebra in 1978.

Ironically, Wagner was not a fan of the Howard pastiches or L. Sprague de Camp and Lin Carter's rewritings of other stories. So in 1977 he put together three volumes of "The Authorised Editions" of the Conan stories for Berkley/Putman. *The Hour of the Dragon*, *The People of the Black Circle* and *Red Nails* collected Howard's Conan stories exactly as they had first appeared in *Weird Tales*.

As the editor observed: "It is intended that this present edition will for the first time present all twenty-one of Robert E. Howard's Conan tales in their original form—with no editorial emendations, no collaborations, no revisions, no pastiches. Unfortunately, at a time when Conan is at a new peak of popularity, too many fans know Conan only through pastiches or as the posturing superhero of the comics. Howard's authentic portrayal of the barbarian from Cimmeria may come as a shock to many."

Unfortunately, due to contractual difficulties, Wagner was only able to reprint eight of Howard's Conan stories, along with his "historical" essay 'The Hyborian Age', before the series was cancelled.

In 1998, the Science Fiction Book Club published all three volumes in an omnibus edition entitled *The Essential Conan*.

"The dead man reeled and fell with him."

The Savage Tales of
Solomon Kane

ROBERT E. HOWARD

Illustrated by
GARY GIANNI

XXVI

"Robert E. Howard's niche among the masters of
fantasy is already secure with his creation of Conan
and Kull and Solomon Kane."

—Donald M. Grant

ALTHOUGH ROBERT E. HOWARD'S fiction continued to
remain in print from publishers all around the world, it
was not until the early 1970s that the first concerted effort was
made to bring his work together under a single, lavishly-illustrated
and produced series.

Having previously released two of Howard's comedic
Westerns, *A Gent from Bear Creek* and *The Pride of Bear Creek*, in
1965 and 1966 respectively, along with the Solomon Kane
collection *Red Shadows* as a limited edition in 1968, Rhode Island
publisher Donald M. Grant reissued the latter book in 1971 at the
start of an ambitious programme of titles which lasted for the next
two decades.

"Robert E. Howard's niche among the masters of fantasy is
already secure with his creation of Conan and Kull and Solomon
Kane," stated the publisher.

Amongst the new collections issued by Grant were *Marchers of
Valhalla* (1972, illustrated by Robert Bruce Acheson), *The Sowers
of Thunder* (1973, illustrated by Roy G. Krenkel), *Tigers of the Sea*
(1974, illustrated by Tim Kirk), *Worms of the Earth* (1974,

illustrated by David Ireland), *Almuric* (1975, illustrated by David Ireland), *Black Vulma's Vengeance & Other Tales of Pirates* (1976, illustrated by Robert James Pailthorpe), *The Iron Man & Other Tales of the Ring* (1976, illustrated by David Ireland), a redesigned edition of *Marchers of Valhalla* (1977, illustrated by Marcus Boas) containing an extra story, *Red Shadows* (1978, with new artwork by Jeff Jones), *The Road of Azrael* (1979, illustrated by Roy G. Krenkel), *Hawks of Outremer* (1979, illustrated by Rob Macintyre and Chris Pappas), *Lord of the Dead* (1981, illustrated by G. Duncan Eagleson) and *Kull* (1985, illustrated by Ned Dameron).

"Of all the books we have been called upon to publish in our four decades as publishers of fantasy," explained Donald M. Grant, "perhaps those tales that recall the exploits of Kull, Robert E. Howard's warrior, outcast, Valusian ruler, have been requested more than any other piece of writing. But despite its obvious popularity, *Kull* has never before been published in a collector's edition, never mind a hardcover book."

Also from Grant, *Red Blades of Black Cathay* (1971) collected three collaborations between Howard and fellow Texan writer Tevis Clyde Smith, only one of which had been published before. Limited to 549 copies, *Singers in the Shadows* (1970) was a collection of twenty poems originally assembled by Howard himself in 1928. This was followed by two further poetry collections, *Echoes from an Iron Harp* (1972, illustrated by Alicia Austin) and *Shadows of Dreams* (1989, illustrated by Richard Berry).

Donald M. Grant also published *The Last Celt: A Bio-Bibliography of Robert Ervin Howard* (1976), a hefty non-fiction volume compiled by the author's literary agent, Glenn Lord. *One Who Walked Alone: Robert E. Howard, The Final Years* (1986) was a fascinating memoir by former Texas schoolteacher Novalyne Price Ellis, who had occasionally dated Howard and kept a series of journals and diaries in which she wrote about her relationship with the author. *Post Oaks & Sand Roughs* (1990) was a previously unpublished, semi-autobiographical main-stream novel that featured thinly-disguised characters, places and publications that Howard knew from his life and the towns in which he lived.

However, perhaps Donald M. Grant's greatest triumph as a publisher was to bring Robert E. Howard's series of Conan stories together in uniformly bound, illustrated deluxe hardcover editions.

Starting in 1974 with *The People of the Black Circle*, which featured interior illustrations and tipped-in colour plates by David Ireland, Grant's impressive Conan reissue programme comprised matched editions of *A Witch Shall Be Born* (1975, illustrated by Alicia Austin), *The Tower of the Elephant* (1975, illustrated by Richard Robertson), *Red Nails* (1975, illustrated by George Barr), *The Devil in Iron* (1976, illustrated by Dan Green), *Rogues in the House* (1976, illustrated by Marcus Boas), *Queen of the Black Coast* (1978, illustrated by Michael Hague), *Black Colossus* (1979, illustrated by Ned Dameron), *Jewels of Gwahlur* (1979, illustrated by Dean Morrissey), *The Pool of the Black One* (1986, illustrated by Hank Jankus) and *The Hour of the Dragon* (1989, illustrated by Ezra Tucker). All these volumes had print runs of around 3,000 copies.

Almost a decade after Donald M. Grant's reprint programme of Howard's books ended, the British publishing firm Wandering Star, co-founded by book designer Marcelo Anciano, launched the first volume in its series "The Wandering Star Robert E. Howard Library of Classics".

The Savage Tales of Solomon Kane (1998) was a stunning volume, collecting all Howard's stories and poems about his dour Puritan swordman. However, what made the book extra special was the copious number of illustrations and colour plates by Chicago artist Gary Gianni.

"I have a confession to make," admitted Gianni. "I never read any of the Solomon Kane stories before I was asked to illustrate them... Granted I never knew Kane, but the spirit he embodies—

that of the romantic hero—ah! Now I'm on fictional terra firma. Robin Hood, Long John Silver, Captain Nemo, Tarzan, not to mention Conan—these are the figures I grew up on. I know them well and along with millions of other readers, have thrilled to their exploits. Solomon Kane is easily part of this tradition."

The book was published in a slipcased and numbered edition of 1,050 copies along with a set of six colour plates and a CD of the poems set to music and read by Paul Blake. It was also available in a leather-bound deluxe edition of fifty copies with even more extras.

Wandering Star's *The Ultimate Triumph: The Heroic Fantasy of Robert E Howard* (1999) was a collection of stories, poems and letters profusely illustrated by Frank Frazetta, while *Bran Mak Morn: The Last King* (2001) was once again illustrated by Gary Gianni and contained all Howard's stories and fragments about the last king of the Picts, along with a number of essays. The limited editions included a CD with a dramatization of the story 'Worms of the Earth'.

In 2002, the imprint launched its most ambitious project to date, *Robert E. Howard's Complete Conan of Cimmeria* with *Volume One (1932–1933)*. As artist Mark Schultz noted, "I discovered Robert E. Howard's Conan in 1969, when I was thirteen years old. I read the stories for their incomparable high adventure and mind-blasting horror... Today I find Conan to be just as compelling a reading experience as I did thirty-two years ago—and now far richer."

Volume Two (1934) followed in 2003 with art by Gary Gianni, and *Volume Three (1935)* in 2009, illustrated by Gregory Manchess. The last volume to date, it was published in collaboration with the Book Palace Bookstore in London.

Wandering Star also published various Robert E. Howard-related sketchbooks by Gary Gianni and Mark Schultz, along with a facsimile typescript of the Conan novella 'The Black Stranger' in 2002, limited to 250 numbered copies signed by Gianni.

"Howard wrote for pulp magazines which are generally not known for their subtle nuances," noted the artist. "But he did write with an unvarnished passion and readers respond to that quality. Isn't that what adventure stories are all about?"

In 2007, Del Rey/Ballantine launched a series of trade paperback reprints of Robert E. Howard's stories with mass-market reprints of the Wandering Star books under the titles *The Coming of Conan the Cimmerian*, *The Savage Tales of Solomon Kane*, *The Bloody Crown of Conan*, *Bran Mak Morn: The Last King* and *The Conquering Sword of Conan*, before extending the series with the original illustrated collections *Kull: Exile of Atlantis* (2006), *The Best of Robert E. Howard. Volume 1: Crimson Shadows* (2007), *The Best of Robert E. Howard Volume 2: Grim Lands* (2007) and *The Horror Stories of Robert E. Howard* (2008).

The latter volume collected sixty stories from *Weird Tales* and other periodicals, and was illustrated by British comics artist Greg Staples, who explained: "Howard is a master of atmosphere and detail, and when I read his stories, I am in them; I can see the buttons on the costumes, smell the dank air, and feel the foreboding."

While he was alive, Howard himself had hinted in letters that he was planning to move away from fantasy fiction, and there has been much conjecture over the years that, had he lived, he would have made his name as a regional writer, with more mainstream stories or histories set in his native Southwest.

In his Foreword to the 1946 Arkham House collection of Howard's short fiction, *Skull-Face and Others*, editor August Derleth supported this view: "The late Robert E. Howard was a writer of pulp fiction. He was also more than that. He had in him the promise of becoming an important American regionalist, and to that end he had been assimilating the lore and legend, the history and culture patterns of his own corner of Texas with a view to writing of them seriously."

We shall never know how he may have developed as a writer. But if he had continued to work in the fantastic field, we can only speculate as to where Howard himself might have taken Conan. In his 1936 letter to P. Schuyler Miller he left behind a number of clues: "He was, I think, king of Aquilonia for many years, in a turbulent and unquiet reign, when the Hyborian civilization had reached its most magnificent high-tide, and every king had imperial ambitions. At first he fought on the defensive, but I am of the opinion that at last he was forced into wars of aggression as a matter of self-preservation. Whether he succeeded in conquering a world-wide empire, or perished in the attempt, I do not know.

"He travelled widely, not only before his kingship, but after he was king. He travelled to Khitai and Hyrkania, and to the even less known regions north of the latter and south of the former. He even visited a nameless continent in the western hemisphere, and roamed among the islands adjacent to it. How much of this roaming will get into print, I can not fortell [*sic*] with any accuracy."

Tragically, because of his suicide, none of it ever did from Howard's imagination.

the
black
stone

by robert e. howard

THE INHABITANT

OF THE LAKE

& LESS WELCOME TENANTS

J. RAMSEY CAMPBELL

utpatel

XXVII

"I've always liked things I didn't understand. It's nice to have the feeling that the world looms larger than is revealed to you by your own perceptions and intelligence."

—Peter Straub

LTHOUGH BY THE early 1950s most of H.P. Lovecraft's original circle of friends and protégés had moved away from the Cthulhu Mythos to develop their own individual writing styles, August Derleth had continued to turn out a steady stream of Lovecraftian pastiches for *Weird Tales* before the magazine ended its initial run with the digest-sized September 1954 issue. After thirty-two years, declining budgets, market conditions and the collapse of its publisher sealed the demise of "The Unique Magazine".

However, a new generation of authors was soon poised to re-invent the Cthulhu Mythos for a modern readership. The first and most notable amongst these newcomers was Liverpool writer (John) Ramsey Campbell who, at the suggestion of Derleth, created an Arkham-like milieu in Britain for his first collection, *The Inhabitant of the Lake and Less Welcome Tenants* (1964), which was published by Arkham House when the author was just eighteen years old.

"When I was fourteen I first encountered H.P. Lovecraft," recalled Campbell. "*Cry Horror!* (1958) was a collection of some of

Lovecraft's best—and worst—stories, and I read it in a day. I immersed myself and decided that this was the greatest stuff I'd ever read and thereupon wrote some Lovecraftian stories to the extent of imitating his style and setting them in Massachusetts when I'd hardly set foot outside Liverpool."

In 1969 August Derleth edited an anthology of these pastiche stories, *Tales of the Cthulhu Mythos*, which included contributions from most of Arkham House's established stable of authors, along with newcomers such as Ramsey Campbell, Colin Wilson and Royal Military Police Sergeant Brian Lumley.

"I was twenty-nine when—having by then collected almost all of the available Lovecraft material—I wrote to August Derleth at Arkham House to order books," explained Lumley. "Along with monies, I sent some 'extracts' from a handful of dubiously titled 'black books', the survivors of antique, now extinct civilizations that either worshipped or shunned the variously imagined 'gods' and 'demons' of the Cthulhu Cycle. These forbidden volumes were my own invention (following in the footsteps of HPL and others) and Derleth seemed much taken by them; he hinted that I might like to 'try my hand' at writing 'something solid in the Mythos' for an anthology he was going to call *Tales of the Cthulhu Mythos*. Of course I attended to that immediately!"

After appearing with several Cthulhu Mythos stories in *Tales of the Cthulhu Mythos* and issues of *The Arkham Collector*, Lumley joined the Arkham House line-up with the collections *The Caller of the Black* (1971) and *The Horror at Oakdeene and Others* (1977), along with the novel *Beneath the Moors* (1974).

"It's hard to name a single modern writer of weird fiction who hasn't to some extent, often profoundly, felt the influence of Howard Phillips Lovecraft," continued Lumley. "It's possible that I personally would never have written anything if I hadn't first read Lovecraft, and I fancy I'm but one of many."

British author Basil Copper's first genre novel, *The Great White*

Space (1974), was dedicated to H.P. Lovecraft and August Derleth—"Openers of the Way". This tale of an expedition to the centre of the Earth was not only inspired by the "Cthulhu Mythos", but was also in the tradition of Arthur Conan Doyle's *The Lost World*.

"I rate Lovecraft very highly indeed and at his very best the next in succession to the great 19th-century master," revealed Copper some years later. "Poe is, of course, now recognised as a classic author both in prose and poetry and, though in a somewhat lower niche, I am certain that Lovecraft will in time—though it may take another thirty years—take his true place as a classic writer in the field he made uniquely his own."

American-born James Wade lived in South Korea and started writing Mythos short stories in the 1940s. However, these didn't appear in print until two decades later and were only eventually collected in 2018—thirty-five years after the author's death—in a volume entitled *Such Things May Be*, which had initially been announced by Arkham House many years earlier but never appeared.

Around 1965, author and editor Lin Carter began writing poetry that included elements of the Cthulhu Mythos and was based on Lovecraft's sonnet cycle 'Fungi from Yuggoth'. *Dreams from R'lyeh* was a slim volume of Carter's verse published by Arkham House in 1975.

Prolific British author Colin Wilson wrote the Mythos-inspired novels *The Mind Parasites* (1967) and *The Philosopher's Stone* (1971), as well as the novella 'The Return of Lloigor' (1969), after he had severely criticised Lovecraft's writing as being "atrocious" in his book *The Strength to Dream* (1962).

"In due course, a copy of my book fell into the hands of August Derleth," explained Wilson, "and Derleth wrote to me, protesting that my judgement of Lovecraft was too harsh, and asking me why, if I was all that good, I didn't try writing a 'Lovecraft' novel myself."

Gary Myers' "fix-up" novel *The House of the Worm* (1975), based on material that was originally serialised in *The Arkham Collector*, was inspired by the title of a novel Lovecraft intended to write for *Weird Tales* back in the early 1920s.

Soon, new single-author collections and anthologies of Lovecraft-inspired work began appearing from major publishing houses and small press imprints all over the world. Lin Carter edited *The Spawn of Cthulhu* (1971), Edward P. Berglund edited *The Disciples of Cthulhu* (1976), Ramsey Campbell edited *New Tales of the Cthulhu Mythos* (1980, which included a new Stephen King novella), and James Turner edited *Tales of the Cthulhu Mythos* (1990) and *Eternal Lovecraft: The Persistence of HPL in Popular Culture* (1998).

Editors Robert E. Weinberg and Martin H. Greenberg celebrated the author's centennial with *Lovecraft's Legacy* (1990). *Shadows Over Innsmouth* (1994), *Weird Shadows Over Innsmouth* (2005) and *Weirder Shadows Over Innsmouth* (2013) were a trilogy of themed anthologies edited by Stephen Jones, while Robert M. Price edited numerous themed volumes for gaming imprint Chaosium, along with such titles as *Tales of the Lovecraft Mythos* (1992), *The New Lovecraft Circle* (1996) and *Acolytes of Cthulhu* (2001).

The Children of Cthulhu (2002) was edited by John Pelan and Benjamin Adams, while Pelan and Michael Reaves' *Shadows Over Baker Street* (2003) combined Lovecraft's themes and characters with Sherlock Holmes. From Kurodahan Press, editor Asamatsu Ken's "Lairs of the Hidden Gods" anthology series, originally published as two volumes (*Hishinkai*) in 2002, offered a unique interpretation of the Cthulhu Mythos from a Japanese perspective.

Since 2010, Lovecraft scholar S.T. Joshi has edited several volumes in his *Black Wings: New Tales of Lovecraftian Horror* series of anthologies, along with numerous non-fiction books about Lovecraft and his work.

Contemporary authors such Donald R. Burleson, Fred Chappell, Neil Gaiman, John Glasby, C.J. Henderson, Caitlín R. Kiernan, T.E.D. Klein, Thomas Ligotti, Richard A. Lupoff, Brian McNaughton, Kim Newman, W.H. Pugmire, Stephen Mark Rainey, Stanley C. Sargent, Mark Samuels and Richard L. Tierney, amongst numerous others, have all taken their inspiration from Lovecraft's works.

Joyce Carol Oates selected *Tales of H.P. Lovecraft*, a "best of" collection of ten stories in 1997. "I'd first read Lovecraft when I was a young adolescent," she recalled, "which is perhaps the best time to read Lovecraft. Now, I admire him for his style, his monomaniacal precision, the 'weirdness' of his imagination, and the underlying, intransigent tragic vision that informs all of his work. He's an American original, whose influences on subsequent writers in the field (Stephen King, for instance) is all-pervasive."

In 2001, *Black Seas of Infinity: The Best of H.P. Lovecraft* contained nineteen stories and three non-fiction pieces, edited by Andrew Wheeler for the Science Fiction Book Club. Best-selling author Peter Straub edited *Lovecraft: Tales* (2005), a classy hardcover collection of twenty-two classic tales published by the prestigious Library of America imprint.

"I read Lovecraft when I was thirteen," recalled Straub. "I didn't understand him, but I thought he was really good. I've always liked things I didn't understand. It's nice to have the feeling that the world looms larger than is revealed to you by your own perceptions and intelligence."

Victor Gollancz had been Lovecraft's hardcover publisher in Britain since the early 1950s, when the publisher wrote to August Derleth to enquire about obtaining the UK rights to some of Lovecraft's stories. Over the next two decades, Gollancz issued sometimes slightly modified editions of *The Haunter of the Dark and Other Tales of Horror* (1951), *The Case of Charles Dexter Ward* (1951), *At the Mountains of Madness and Other Tales of Terror*

(1966), *Dagon and Other Macabre Tales* (1967) and *The Shadow Out of Time and Other Tales of Horror* (which also contained several "posthumous collaborations" by Derleth, 1968), along with *The Lurker at the Threshold* (1968), all in their distictive yellow dust jackets.

Gollancz finally brought together all of H.P. Lovecraft's major fiction in two collections, *Necronomicon: The Weird Tales of H.P. Lovecraft* (2008) and *Eldritch Tales: A Miscellany of the Macabre* (2011), both compiled by Stephen Jones and illustrated by Les Edwards.

"Somehow Lovecraft has become permanent," explained the artist. "He endures. Even the word 'Lovecraftian' has slipped into the language, although there might be strange ambiguities as to what it actually means. For some it refers to the literary style, for others it's to do with bulging gelatinous masses, the chanting of barbarous names and huge, ancient and tentacled beings. It's why the best of Lovecraft's stories are worth returning to."

The publisher decided to utilise the "classic" texts created by Arkham House and *Weird Tales*, but made a number of corrections and revisions based on the vast amounts of research that has been done by Lovecraft scholars (especially S.T. Joshi) over the previous two decades.

H.P. Lovecraft himself turned up as a character in such revisionist novels as *Pulptime* (1984) by Peter H. Cannon (alongside Sherlock Holmes, Harry Houdini and Frank Belknap Long, Jr.); *Lovecraft's Book* (1985) by Richard A. Lupoff (featuring many of the "Lovecraft Circle" of writers battling the Nazis); *Shadows Bend: A Novel of the Fantastic and Unspeakable* (2000) by David Barbour and Richard Raleigh (teaming HPL with fellow *Weird Tales* authors Robert E. Howard and Clark Ashton Smith); *The Arcanum* (2004), a debut novel by Thomas Wheeler (involving Sir Arthur Conan Doyle, Harry Houdini and voodoo priestess Marie Laveau), and *The Chinese Death Cloud Peril* (2006) by Paul

Malmont (in which pulp magazine authors Walter Gibson, Lester Dent and L. Ron Hubbard investigated Lovecraft's horrifying poisoning).

Matt Ruff's *Lovecraft Country* (2016) was a "fix-up" novel of eight interconnected stories which attempted to link H.P. Lovecraft's fiction with racism in the United States during the late 1950s and early '60s. In 2020 it was adapted into a ten-episode TV series on HBO.

Peter Cannon's collection *Scream for Jeeves: A Parody* (1994) contained three Lovecraftian tales featuring P.G. Wodehouse's Jeeves and Wooster, and Nick Mamatas' debut novel *Move Under Ground* (2004) involved "Beat Era" authors Jack Kerouac, Neal Cassady, Alan Ginsberg and William S. Burroughs battling the minions of Lovecraft's Cthulhu Mythos in the California of the early 1960s.

By now it had become apparent that no genre was safe, or any plot too outlandish, when it came to authors putting a new spin on H.P. Lovecraft and his work.

However, perhaps Ramsey Campbell summed it up best when he said, "H.P. Lovecraft is the most important single writer of the weird...his achievement lies not so much in his influence as in the enduring qualities of his finest work."

Ballantine Books 02427·3·095

Lovecraft: A Look Behind The "Cthulhu Mythos"

The background of a Myth that has captured a generation.

Lin Carter

XXVIII

"Lovecraft, I suggest, never took himself as seriously
as do the idolators who have made him a cult-object."
—E. Hoffman Price

OR MANY YEARS, August Derleth was acknowledged as
the foremost authority on Lovecraft with his introductions to
various collections of the author's work. New York publisher Ben
Abramson issued Derleth's *H.P.L.: A Memoir* in 1945 as a slim
hardcover volume of 1,000 copies. A further study, *Some Notes on
H.P. Lovecraft*, appeared as a 1,044-copy chapbook under the
Arkham House imprint in 1959, while in 1963 Derleth annotated
Lovecraft's *Autobiography of a Nonentity*, which was published for
Arkham by the Villiers Press in England as a 500-copy booklet.

California's The Futile Press had produced *The Notes &
Commonplace Book Employed by the Late H.P. Lovecraft* in 1938 as
a forty-eight-page booklet prepared by R.H. Barlow, and *Lovecraft:
A Symposium* (1964) was a transcription of a discussion between
Arthur Jean Cox, Robert Bloch, Fritz Leiber, Sam Russell and
Leland Sapiro, recorded at the October 24, 1963 meeting of the Los
Angeles Science Fantasy Society (LASFS).

As a companion to his influential "Adult Fantasy" series for
Ballantine Books, Lin Carter's ground-breaking study *Lovecraft: A
Look Behind the "Cthulhu Mythos"* (1972) presented details of its

subject's life and works to a general readership for the first time. It was followed by *Howard Phillips Lovecraft: Dreamer on the Nightside* (1975) by Frank Belknap Long, *Lovecraft at Last* (1975) by Willis Conover, and L. Sprague de Camp's controversial *Lovecraft: A Biography* (1975). French writer Michel Houellebecq's long essay *H.P. Lovecraft: Contre le monde, contre le vie* (aka *H.P. Lovecraft: Against the World, Against Life*, 1991) was equally disputable.

Anybody looking for a definitive biography of the author could do no better than pick up a copy of *H.P.Lovecraft: A Life* (1996) by renowned Lovecraft authority S.T. Joshi, while *Lovecraft Remembered* (1998), edited by Peter Cannon for Arkham House, was a thorough collection of reminiscences and memoirs by friends and fellow writers.

"Lovecraft, I suggest, never took himself as seriously as do the idolators who have made him a cult-object," succinctly observed his friend and correspondent E. Hoffman Price.

In recent years, Lovecraft scholarship has been boosted to an almost pathological level, and writers such as Joshi have created entire careers around dissecting the minutiae of the author's literary output. This has led to a burgeoning industry of specialty press titles dedicated to Lovecraft's life and works. Along with such fan publications as *Book of Dark Wisdom: The Magazine of Dark Fiction and Lovecraftian Horror*, Robert M. Price's *Crypt of Cthulhu, Cthulhu Codex, Cthulhu Sex, Dagon*, Joshi's *Lovecraft Studies, Lovecraft's Weird Mysteries, Midnight Shambler, Mythos Collector, Nyctalops* and *Tales of Lovecraftian Horror*, to name only a few. *H.P. Lovecraft's Magazine of Horror* was a short-lived fiction periodical launched in 2003 by Wildside Press, while Stephen Jones' *H.P. Lovecraft in Britain* (2007) was a 750-copy chapbook that concentrated on the author's parallel career in the UK.

The first World Fantasy Convention was held in Lovecraft's home city of Providence, Rhode Island, in October 1975. Aimed specifically at professionals and collectors in the field, its objective was to celebrate "The Lovecraft Circle" of friends and colleagues from *Weird Tales* and Arkham House.

The Guest of Honour at the initial gathering was Robert Bloch, with artist Gahan Wilson as Toastmaster for the World Fantasy Awards.

It became an annual event the following year, and subsequent guests included such genre veterans as C.L. Moore, Richard Matheson, Fritz Leiber, Frank Belknap Long, Joseph Payne Brennan, Manly Wade Wellman, Evangeline Walton, Frank Kelly Freas, L. Sprague de Camp, Julius Schwartz, Hugh B. Cave, Jack Williamson and Glenn Lord.

Lovecraftian academicism perhaps reached its highest point in 1990, when the H.P. Lovecraft Centennial Conference was held at Brown University in Providence, Rhode Island.

MythosCon was a horror convention dedicated to H.P. Lovecraft and the Cthulhu Mythos. It was held in Phoenix, Arizona, in January 2011 with Ramsey Campbell as the Guest of Honour. Although further events were planned, it remained a one-off event.

The bi-annual NecronomiCon Providence was a part-academic gathering launched in August 2013 to explore the life and works of Lovecraft and other creators of weird fiction, film and art of the past and the present.

The annual H.P. Lovecraft Film Festival was started in Portland, Oregon, in October 1996 by Andrew Migliore so that Lovecraft could be rightly recognised as a master of Gothic horror and his work more faithfully adapted to film and television. "I have found that student and amateur films are far more faithful to the spirit of Lovecraft and his macabre stories," explained Migliore.

More recently, a second festival has alternated every other year with NecronomiCon in Providence.

A TIMESCAPE

CLARK ASHTON SMITH
THE CITY OF THE SINGING FLAME

THE BEST IN FANTASY AND HORROR BY ONE OF THE TWENTIETH CENTURY'S GREATS!

Rowena

XXIX

"He filled my mind with incredible worlds,
impossibly beautiful cities, and still more fantastic
creatures."

—Ray Bradbury

I N 1965, CALIFORNIAN poet and scholar Donald Sidney-Fryer
compiled and introduced *Poems in Prose* for Arkham House.
Limited to 1,016 copies, it collected all but one of Clark Ashton
Smith's prose poems. An early voice in the critical recognition of the
author's work, Sidney-Fryer also assembled the Arkham House
collection *Other Dimensions*, published in 1970 in an edition of 3,114
copies. It contained twenty-six stories—most of Smith's published
fiction not included in previous Arkham House volumes.

1970 also saw the first mass-market paperback editions of
Smith's work. Following the revival in interest of H.P. Lovecraft and
Robert E. Howard's work in the late 1960s, editor Lin Carter
compiled the collections *Zothique* (1970), *Hyperborea* (1971),
Xiccarph (1972) and *Poseidonis* (1973) for his renowned "Adult
Fantasy" series from Ballantine Books.

Meanwhile, Roy Squires released "The Fugitive Poems of Clark
Ashton Smith" in 1970, comprising *The Tartarus of the Suns, The
Palace of Jewels, In the Ultimate Valleys* and *To George Sterling: Five
Poems*. An extremely limited series of four pamphlets which he
hand-printed from hand-set type on quality papers, this first set

of poems from Squires were early work which Smith had not selected for *The Star-Treader* and had remained unpublished until then.

'The Mortuary', Smith's only prose poem to have been inadvertently left out of the Arkham House collection *Poems in Prose*, appeared as a hand-printed pamphlet of 180 copies from Squires in 1971.

Although Smith had originally submitted the manuscript to Arkham House back in 1949, Derleth was only persuaded to finally publish *Selected Poems* (1971) when the author's widow, Carolyn Wakefield, offered to underwrite the $1,700.00 printing and binding costs out of the advances she received from the Ballantine paperbacks. Mrs. Wakefield asked Squires to send Arkham a copy of the charcoal drawing of Smith by Natalie Bixby Carter, which was used on the dust wrapper.

Edited by Donald Sidney-Fryer, *Selected Poems* was one of the last books sent to the printer by Derleth before he died in July 1971. The 400-page collection was published a few months after his death in an edition of 2,118 copies, exorbitantly priced (for Arkham) at $10.00.

Roy Squires published the prose poem *Sadastor* in 1972 in an edition of 108 copies, and he included a colour pen and wash drawing by Smith in the 198-copy edition of another prose poem, *From the Crypts of Memory* (1973).

That same year, collector and publisher Gerry de la Ree issued the first compilation of drawings by Smith, *Grotesques and Fantastiques*. The 600-copy booklet also included previously unpublished poems sent to fellow poet Samuel Loveman, which Smith probably considered minor pieces. From the same publisher, *Klarkash-Ton and Monstro Ligriv* (1974) included previously unpublished poems, art and correspondence between Smith and illustrator Virgil Finlay. It was limited to 500 copies.

Clark Ashton Smith: Artist (1975) was a twelve-page stapled pamphlet produced by de la Ree for The Hyborean League in an edition of around 100 copies or less. It included excerpts from Smith's letters to Loveman about the artwork he was working on at the time.

With interest in Smith's work steadily increasing, in 1973 Mirage Press published both the author's *Planets and Dimensions: Collected Essays* and Dennis Rickard's heavily illustrated *The Fantastic Art of Clark Ashton Smith*.

For his second selection of "The Fugitive Poems of Clark Ashton Smith", Roy Squires used poems which had been written after the manuscript for *Selected Poems* had been prepared back in 1948. *The Titans of Tartarus* (1974), *A Song from Hell* (1975), *The Potion of Dreams* (1975), *The Fanes of Dawn* (1976), *Seer of the Cycles* (1976) and *The Burden of the Suns* (1977) were printed in both ordinary and large-paper states. Subscribers to these latter "Manuscript Editions" each received one of around fifty holograph poems, either handwritten or typed and signed by Smith, which were included with their set of booklets.

Prince Alcouz and the Magician (1977) was published by Squires in an edition of 190 copies. As with many of Smith's early stories, it included a thread of Orientalism, which had fascinated the author in his younger years. Obviously inspired by his love of the *Arabian Nights*, this very early work revealed an exoticism and sardonic humour which Smith retained in his more mature writing.

In 1977, The Clark Ashton Smith Papers Collection was donated by Smith's son-in-law and literary executor Richard E. Kuhn to the John Hay Library of Brown University, Providence, Rhode Island—where H.P. Lovecraft's papers are also stored. A second batch of manuscripts, letters and miscellaneous papers were delivered in 1981.

However, at least five stories known to have been completed by Smith and dating from the 1930s, are apparently lost. Two of the tales were handed over to E. Hoffman Price, who totally rewrote them. They were published as 'Dawn of Discord' and 'The Old Gods Eat' (aka 'House of the Monoceros') in the October 1940 and February 1941 issues, respectively, of *Spicy Mystery Stories*. Although Smith was not credited, Price paid his friend two-thirds of the fees he received.

Donald Sidney-Fryer published his comprehensive volume *Emperor of Dreams: A Clark Ashton Smith Bibliography* through Donald M. Grant in 1978. Along with listings of poems, prose, first line indices, juvenilia, translations and pseudonyms, the 1,500-copy edition also included letters from such acquaintances as Fritz Leiber, Ray Bradbury, August Derleth, H. Warner Munn and Harlan Ellison, plus numerous photographs of the author.

Shortly after Smith's death in 1961, Sidney-Fryer and Rah Hoffman (a friend of the writer since the early 1940s and co-editor of the amateur magazine *The Acolyte*) obtained the author's black leather notebook from his widow. From around 1929 onwards, Smith had maintained this book, in which he would jot down miscellaneous ideas, themes, words or names for possible future use. Some of these notes had already appeared in *The Acolyte* in 1944.

By March 1962, Sidney-Fryer and Hoffman had deciphered, transcribed, prepared and proofread a text which reproduced the literary contents of Smith's commonplace book at the time of his death. It was eventually published by Arkham House in 1979 as *The Black Book of Clark Ashton Smith*. Issued in an edition of just over 2,500 copies with interior illustrations by Andrew Smith, the softcover volume was bound in simulated black-leather covers in an attempt to fabricate the appearance of the author's original notebook.

Sidney-Fryer also edited a new series of mass-market paperback collections by Smith for Pocket Books' Timescape imprint, comprising *The City of the Singing Flame* (1981), *The Last Incantation* (1982) and *The Monster of the Prophecy* (1983).

As it is Written, a purportedly lost work by Smith writing as "DeLysle Ferrée Cass" and published by Donald M. Grant in 1982, was subsequently revealed to be by another author entirely.

Much of Smith's overtly erotic and elaborate prose was often cut by the pulp editors (especially those working for the Gernsback science fiction magazines), yet for some reason the author never got around to restoring the text for the book reprintings. This was probably because, according to Roy Squires, Smith—like Lovecraft—"would, whenever feasible, avoid typing a manuscript". The stories he submitted to Arkham House for his collections usually consisted of tearsheets from the magazines, thus perpetuating any errors or omissions in those versions.

Although many of the author's original manuscripts had been destroyed in the fire set by vandals back in 1957, carbon copies of around two-thirds of his published stories survived amongst his papers. In the late 1980s, Necronomicon Press issued a series of chapbooks under the title "The Unexpurgated Clark Ashton Smith" that included a few of these surviving original texts. Edited by Steve Behrends, the series featured *Mother of Toads* (1987), *The Dweller in the Gulf* (1987, originally published in 1933 as 'The Dweller in the Martian Depths'), *The Monster of the Prophecy* (1988), *The Vaults of Yoh-Vombis* (1988), *The Witchcraft of Ulua* (1988) and *Xeethra* (1988).

Klarkash-Ton: The Journal of Smith Studies was a scholarly periodical published between 1988–93, changing its title to *The Dark Eidolon* for the final two issues.

Necronomicon also published *Clark Ashton Smith: Letters to H.P. Lovecraft* (1987), also edited by Behrends, and *Nostalgia of the Unknown: The Complete Prose Poetry of Clark Ashton Smith* (1988), edited by Marc and Susan Michaud, Behrends and S.T. Joshi.

Having survived August Derleth's death and prospered over the years under various editorial hands, in 1988 Arkham House finally got around to publishing the book it had previously announced as *The Best Fantastic Tales of Clark Ashton Smith. A Rendezvous in Averoigne* contained thirty stories set in Smith's various lost worlds, embellished by Jeffrey K. Potter's photo-illustrations.

"He filled my mind with incredible worlds, impossibly beautiful cities, and still more fantastic creatures," Ray Bradbury recalled in his short introduction.

The following year, Steve Behrends, Donald Sidney-Fryer and Rah Hoffman edited *Strange Shadows: The Uncollected Fiction and Essays of Clark Ashton Smith* for Greenwood Press. With an introduction by Robert Bloch, the book contained Smith's final completed stories, plus variant versions, fragments, synopses, prose poems, plays and various miscellaneous material (some of which had originally appeared in the magazine *Crypt of Cthulhu 27: Untold Tales* in 1984).

Amongst this previously uncollected material was the story 'A Good Embalmer', which Smith had written in 1931. As he explained in a letter to August Derleth in February that same year: "I have spent three days over a six-page horror. It is not my natural genre, and may not even have the dubious merit of being salable [*sic*]". Smith may have been unhappy with the result and decided to publish it under a pseudonym. Three years later, *The Fantasy Fan* announced that 'The Embalmers of Ramsville' by Michael Weir would appear in a forthcoming issue. However, the tale was never published.

Necronomicon Press issued *The Hashish-Eater* in 1989, illustrated by Robert H. Knox; and an annotated edition of the poem, limited to less than thirty copies, was given to audience members when Donald Sidney-Fryer performed a dramatic reading of the original version of the work on November 24, 1990.

The Devil's Notebook: Collected Epigrams and Pensées was edited by Don Herron and appeared from Ted Dikty's Starmont House as both a trade paperback and hardcover in 1990. It reprinted many of the witty and philosophical epigrams Smith had published over the years in his newspaper column for the *Auburn Journal*. Meanwhile, Steve Behrends' *Clark Ashton Smith* (1990) appeared as the Starmont Readers Guide #49.

A Prophecy of Monsters (1995) was a 100-copy chapbook from 13th Hour Books that reprinted Smith's story (later retitled 'Monsters in the Night') from *The Magazine of Fantasy & Science Fiction* in 1954.

Recorded in the late 1950s by Robert B. Elder, in 1995 Necronomicon Press released *Live from Auburn: The Elder Tapes*, a cassette of Clark Ashton Smith actually reading eleven of his poems along with an accompanying booklet containing the texts.

From the same publisher, *Tales of Zothique* (1995) was a trade paperback edited by Will Murray and Steve Behrends that collected all Smith's Zothique tales, using fragments and original manuscripts, along with the play 'The Dead Will Cuckold You'.

The volume was a success, and the following year Necronomicon issued *The Book of Hyperboria* (1996), edited by Will Murray and featuring corrected texts based on Smith's original manuscripts, including an unabridged version of 'The Coming of the White Worm'.

The Emperor of Dreams: The Lost Worlds of Clark Ashton Smith was a representative collection of the author's stories edited by Stephen Jones and published in 2002 as part of Gollancz's "Fantasy Masterworks" series.

In 2020, Hippocampus Press published *Clark Ashton Smith: A Comprehensive Bibliography* compiled by Scott Connors, S.T. Joshi and David E. Schultz, while Joshi and Schultz had also edited *The Shadow of the Unattained: The Letters of George Sterling and Clark Ashton Smith* (2005) and *Dawnward Spire, Lonely Hill: The Letters of H. P. Lovecraft and Clark Ashton Smith* (2017) and for the same imprint.

What was the hideous thing in the PIT
that came to honor her?
AMERICAN INTERNATIONAL presents
EDGAR ALLAN POE'S
THE
Haunted
PALACE
in PATHÉCOLOR AND PANAVISION®
STARRING
VINCENT PRICE
DEBRA PAGET
LON CHANEY
Produced and Directed by ROGER CORMAN · Screenplay by CHARLES BEAUMONT · Executive Producers: JAMES H. NICHOLSON and SAMUEL Z. ARKOFF

XXX

"I shall never permit anything bearing my signature
to be banalised and vulgarised into the infantile
twaddle which passes for 'horror tales' amongst
radio and cinema audiences!"
—H.P. Lovecraft

I T WAS INEVITABLE that as H.P. Lovecraft's popularity
increased, so his work would be adapted into other media.

Although Lovecraft enjoyed seeing movies (the 1933 time-travel romance *Berkeley Square* was one of his favourites), he did not have a very high opinion of the cinema industry: "Virtually all so-called weird films are simply infantile nonsense," he told Willis Conover.

"I shall never permit anything bearing my signature to be banalised and vulgarised into the infantile twaddle which passes for 'horror tales' amongst radio and cinema audiences!" Lovecraft famously wrote in a 1933 letter.

The first official adaptation of the author's work on film was American International Picture's *The Haunted Palace* (1963), starring horror film icons Vincent Price and Lon Chaney, Jr. Based on the author's posthumously-published short novel 'The Case of Charles Dexter Ward', the movie actually took its title from the eponymous poem by one of Lovecraft's favourite authors, Edgar Allan Poe.

"I fought against calling it a Poe film," director Roger Corman recalled, "but AIP had made so much money with Poe films that they just stuck his name on it for box-office appeal. To me, I was just making a Lovecraft picture."

Veteran actor Boris Karloff returned to his native Britain to star in *Monster of Terror* (aka *Die Monster Die!*, 1965), director Daniel Haller's loose version of 'The Colour Out of Space', and despite top-billing Americans Gig Young and Carol Lynley, David Greene's *The Shuttered Room* (1966) was also filmed in England. Based on one of Derleth's "posthumous collaborations", a young Oliver Reed portrayed sadistic thug Ethan Whateley. However, there was not a Lovecraftian "Deep One" in sight.

Despite starring such horror heavyweights as Boris Karloff, Christopher Lee, Barbara Steele and Michael Gough, almost nothing remained of an uncredited Jerry Sohl's adaptation of 'The Dreams in the Witch-House' in Vernon Sewell's *Curse of the Crimson Altar* (aka *The Crimson Cult*, 1968). Meanwhile, former teen star Sandra Dee found herself about to be sacrificed to The Great Old Ones by Dean Stockwell's Wilbur Whateley in Daniel Haller's updated psychedelic version of *The Dunwich Horror* (1969), which author and Lovecraft biographer L. Sprague de Camp summed up as "While not bad fun, the movie came nowhere near the original in force".

With Stuart Gordon's outrageously gory *Re-Animator* (1985), loosely based on 'Herbert West—Reanimator', Lovecraft's work received something of a cinematic revival over the following decade. "Compared with Lovecraft's other work, it's a very explicit story, very action-packed," explained Gordon. "The problem with Lovecraft is that he often gets into this 'unspeakable and indescribable horror' stuff, which is hard to portray on screen."

The director's next Lovecraft adaptation, *From Beyond* (1986), fell squarely into that category as Gordon was reunited with his *Re-Animator* stars Jeffrey Combs and Barbara Crampton, who this time transformed into a brain-eating monster.

Combs and Crampton also turned up in a version of Lovecraft's 'The Evil Clergyman', which was included as one of three stories in Charles Band's *Pulse Pounders* (1988), although its release was shelved for many years due to the collapse of the production company that made it.

Directed by actor David Keith, *The Curse* (1987) was another version of 'The Colour Out of Space', while Mark Kinsey Stephenson portrayed a contemporary Randolph Carter in Jean-Paul Ouellette's *The Unnamable* (1988). The actor reprised his role in the same director's 1992 sequel *Unnamable II: The Statement of Randolf Carter* (aka *The Unnamable Returns*).

"As a filmmaker, I've often gone to Lovecraft to get inspiration," revealed Brian Yuzna, director of the sequels *Bride of Re-Animator* (aka *Re-Animator 2*, 1989) and *Beyond Re-Animator* (2003), "and when you read Lovecraft I would defy you to tell me exactly what the story is about. It's very elusive, but the feelings of dread and horror are always there, and very palpably so."

Despite having the film taken away from him during post-production, Dan O'Bannon's *The Resurrected* (1991) remains an impressive modern adaptation of 'The Case of Charles Dexter Ward' starring Chris Sarandon in the dual roles. H.P. Lovecraft himself (in the guise of Jeffrey Combs) turned up to link the anthology movie *Necronomicon* (1993), directed by Christophe Gans, Shusuke Kaneko and Brian Yuzna. Two of the three episodes were loosely based on 'Cool Air' and 'The Whisperer in Darkness'.

Combs continued his connection with Lovecraft films with roles in C. Courtney Joyner's *Lurking Fear* (1994), filmed in Romania, and Stuart Gordon's *Castle Freak* (1995), shot in Italy and loosely inspired by both 'The Outsider' and 'The Shuttered Room'. The latter movie was remade in 2020 and set in Albania.

Although never credited as such, Peter Svatek's *Bleeders* (aka *Hemoglobin*, 1996) was also based on 'The Lurking Fear' (only previously filmed two years earlier). Rutger Hauer played a drunken doctor who saved an island community from ghouls. Stuart Gordon's Spanish-made *Dagon* (aka *Dagon—La secta del mar*, 2001) may have contained elements of Lovecraft's title story, but it was actually the director's long-planned version of 'The Shadow Over Innsmouth'.

From Italy, Ivan Zuccon's shot-on-video *The Shunned House* (2003) combined incomprehensible adaptations of the title story, 'The Music of Eric [*sic*] Zann' and 'The Dreams in the Witch-House', which would have had H.P. Lovecraft spinning in his grave. Barrett J. Leigh and Thom Maurer's *Beyond the Wall of Sleep* (2004) had even less to do with its source material, while Serge Rodnunsky's *Chill* (2006) starring James Russo, Thomas Calabro and Ashley Laurence, was a contemporary reworking of 'Cool Air' set in Los Angeles.

Dean Stockwell, who had starred in the 1969 version, played Dr. Henry Armitage, while Jeffrey Combs was Wilbur Whateley in Leigh Scott's TV movie remake of *The Dunwich Horror* (2008). A German remake of *The Color Out of Space (Die Farbe*, 2010) was a far better interpretation of the author's work, as was *Banshee Chapter* (2013), a contemporary reworking of 'From Beyond'.

Probably nobody was expecting *Call Girl of Cthulhu* (2014), which was the runner-up in the 2012 H.P. Lovecraft Film Festival Screenplay Competition, or the children's cartoons *Howard Lovecraft and the Frozen Kingdom* (2016), *Howard Lovecraft and the Undersea Kingdom* (2017) and *Howard Lovecraft and the Kingdom of Madness* (2018), which were based on graphic novels. Jeffrey Combs voiced the adult Lovecraft in the latter.

Perhaps the most interesting Lovecraft movie adaptation in recent years has been Richard Stanley's psychadelic version of *Color Out of Space* (2019), starring Nicolas Cage and Joely Richardson. A self-described occultist, Stanley brought a real sense of mystery and magic to his version.

Unfortunately, although this was supposed to be the first of three Lovecraftian adaptations (with *The Dunwich Horror* to follow), that trilogy was cancelled in 2021 after a former partner accused the director of domestic abuse.

Lovecraftian references could also be found in such films as Harvey Hart's TV pilot *Dark Intruder* (1965), Lucio Fulci's *City of the Living Dead* (aka *La paura nella citta dei morti viventi/The Gates of Hell*, 1980) and *The Beyond* (aka *E tu vivrai nel terrore... l'aldila/Seven Doors to Death*, 1981), Martin Campbell's inventive TV movie *Cast a Deadly Spell* (1991), J.P. Simon's *Black Magic Mansion* (aka *La mansión de los cthulhu/Cthulhu Mansion*, 1992), John Carpenter's *In the Mouth of Madness* (1994), Ivan Zuccon's *The Darkness Beyond* (aka *L'altrove*, 2000) and *The Unknown Beyond* (aka *Maelstrom, Il Figlio Dell'Altrove*) and even Guillermo del Toro's *Hellboy* (2004), to name just a few titles.

"His use of suggestion and allusion might seem beyond the reach of most filmmakers," observed Ramsey Campbell, "but I submit *The Blair Witch Project* (1998) as the most Lovecraftian of films, not least in the documentary realism he urged upon serious artists in the field and in the inexplicitness with which it conveys, to use his phrase, dread suspense."

Numerous short movies have been made from Lovecraft's stories, many of them quite effective despite the low budgets. One of the most impressive film adaptations of the author's work to date is Andrew Leman's *The Call of Cthulhu* (2005), a silent short filmed in "MythoScope" by the H.P. Lovecraft Historical Society.

"It's as faithful an adaptation of a tale of Lovecraft's as we've yet seen in the cinema," wrote Ramsey Campbell.

Although Lovecraft died before it became a household fixture, he revealed in a letter to Clark Ashton Smith that he had seen an "interesting" demonstration of television in a local department store in 1933. However, despite the obvious advantages of adapting the author's short stories to the small screen, there have been precious few TV versions of his work.

Rod Serling's Night Gallery was an anthology series that ran on NBC-TV from 1970–73. Each story was represented by a macabre painting and introduced by host/creator Serling (of *Twilight Zone* fame). In December 1971 the show presented Lovecraft's 'Pickman's Model', directed by Jack Laird and starring Bradford Dillman as the 19th-century artist who painted from life. The following week, Serling himself adapted 'Cool Air', which was directed by Jeannot Szwarc and featured Henry Darrow as a scientist who had managed to cheat death by keeping cold.

The previous month, the show had presented director Jerrold Freedman's fun-filled 'Professor Peabody's Last Lecture', in which the eponymous teacher (Carl Reiner) debunked The Great Old Ones in front of a class that included students Bloch (Richard Annis), Heald (Louise Lawson), Derleth (Larry Watson) and a geeky Lovecraft (Johnnie Collins, III).

ABC-TV's *The Real Ghostbusters* was a children's cartoon series based on the 1984 movie *Ghostbusters*. In the 1987 episode 'The Collect Call of Cathulhu' [*sic*], scripted by Michael Reaves, the Ghostbusters teamed up with the Miskatonic University's occult scientist Alice Derleth to recover a stolen copy of the *Necronomicon* before it could be used by an ancient cult to open a dimensional portal for the Great Old Ones.

Stuart Gordon was an obvious choice to direct a modern reworking of 'Dreams in the Witch House' (2005) for the first season of the Showtime Network's anthology series *Masters of Horror*.

'Dreams in the Witch House' was also adapted for the Netflix anthology series *Guillermo del Toro's Cabinet of Curiosities* (2022), along with 'Pickman's Model', with varying success. At least the latter episode benifitted from a suitably twitchy performance from Crispin Glover as artist Richard Upton Pickman.

There have of course been television adaptations of Lovecraft's work all over the world, including 'The Shadow Out of Time' in West

Germany (1975), 'The Thing on the Doorstep' in Italy (1982), 'The Shadow Over Innsmouth' in Japan (1992) and 'Pickman's Model' in Chile (2000).

The Case of Howard Phillips Lovecraft was a 1999 French document-ary about the author, while a Canadian biography made the following year, *Out of Mind: The Stories of H.P. Lovecraft*, cast Christopher Heyerdahl as the author and Art Kitching as Randolph Carter.

In 2006, Night Shade Books reissued Andrew Migliore and John Strysik's wide-ranging 1995 study *Lurker in the Lobby: A Guide to the Cinema of H.P. Lovecraft* in a redesigned and updated edition with a Preface by the ubiquitous S.T. Joshi.

In recent years there have been numerous short films and video games based on or inspired by the author's work. However, it has often been argued that horror is more effective when it is heard and not seen. This may be especially true of the works of H.P. Lovecraft.

Possibly the first media adaptation of one of the author's stories was a special Halloween presentation of 'The Dunwich Horror' on the CBS radio show *Suspense*. Hosted by Hollywood star Ronald Colman, it was broadcast on November 1, 1945 and subsequently repeated on Armed Forces Radio.

Since then, Lovecraft's fiction has been widely adapted for audio, including *Fungi from Yuggoth: A Sonnet Cycle*, which was the first release from specialty publisher Fedogan & Bremer in 1989.

In 2001, Britain's Rainfall Records released *Strange Aeons*, a two-disc CD collection inspired by Lovecraft and the Cthulhu Mythos. This audio anthology was produced and directed by artist Steve Lines and featured contributions from writers Ramsey Campbell, Brian Lumley, Simon Clark, Joel Lane, Robert M. Price and Tim Lebbon.

Written and directed by Julian Simpson for BBC Radio 4, *The*

Lovecraft Investigations comprised a series of three podcasts broadcast between January 2019 and November 2020. 'The Case of Charles Dexter Ward', 'The Whisperer in Darkness' and 'The Shadow Over Innsmouth' followed investigators Matt Heawood (Barnaby Kay) and Kennedy Fisher (Jana Carpenter) in modernised versions of original Lovecraft tales.

During the 1960s there was a psychedelic rock group from Chicago called H.P. Lovecraft, whose songs included 'The White Ship' (1967) and 'At the Mountains of Madness' (1969). The band split up after vocalist Dave Michael left to return to university, but they briefly reformed and changed their name to simply Lovecraft, releasing two albums in the early 1970s.

Taking their name from Lovecraft's story 'The Tomb', comedy Canadian band The Darkest of the Hillside Thickets was formed in 1992 and has recorded such albums as *Cthulhuriffomania!* (1994), *Cthulhu Strikes Back* (1995), *The Great Old Ones* (1996) and *The Shadow Out of Tim* (2007).

In December 2006, BBC Radio 3 broadcast *Weird Tales—The Strange Life of H.P. Lovecraft*. Geoff Ward, professor of literature at Dundee University, presented the forty-five-minute show about the influential author that included contributions from Neil Gaiman, S.T. Joshi, Kelly Link, Peter Straub and China Miéville.

THIEF
WARRIOR
GLADIATOR
KING

CONAN
THE BARBARIAN

DINO DE LAURENTIIS PRESENTS

AN EDWARD R. PRESSMAN PRODUCTION

ARNOLD SCHWARZENEGGER · JAMES EARL JONES IN

"CONAN THE BARBARIAN"

STARRING SANDAHL BERGMAN · BEN DAVIDSON · GERRY LOPEZ · MAKO · WILLIAM SMITH AND MAX VON SYDOW AS King Osric

WRITTEN BY JOHN MILIUS AND OLIVER STONE   MUSIC BY BASIL POLEDOURIS   ASSOCIATE PRODUCER EDWARD SUMMER   EXECUTIVE PRODUCERS D. CONSTANTINE CONTE AND EDWARD R. PRESSMAN

PRODUCED BY BUZZ FEITSHANS AND RAFFAELLA DE LAURENTIIS   DIRECTED BY JOHN MILIUS   A UNIVERSAL RELEASE   © 1982 UNIVERSAL CITY STUDIOS, INC.

XXXI

"Milius had no real interest in collaboration. He took
what he wanted from my script, characters and sets,
and made it into a strange hybrid of a spaghetti
Western and a sword and sandals saga."

—Oliver Stone

T HE FIRST, AND to date *only*, television adaptation of a
Robert E. Howard horror story was a superbly atmospheric
version of 'Pigeons from Hell' (originally published in *Weird Tales*,
May 1938), which was initially broadcast on June 6, 1961 on NBC's
anthology series *Thriller*, hosted by Boris Karloff.

In 1982, director John Milius, along with co-writer Oliver
Stone, turned *Conan the Barbarian* into a multi-million-dollar
fantasy movie, with Austrian bodybuilder and former Mr. Universe
Arnold Schwarzenegger cast as the eponymous sword-wielding
hero pitted against James Earl Jones' evil shape-changing sorcerer,
Thulsa Doom.

"I wanted all the magic to be natural, so the audience won't
say, 'Oh, a special effects sequence,'" Milius told James Steranko in
an interview in *Prevue* #48 (1982). "I felt the magic should be
another facet of life in Conan's time. If somebody takes a snake and
turns it into an arrow, no big deal! That's simply part of the culture.

"Whenever Howard wrote his big sorcery sequences,"
continued Milius, "it was usually because he found no other way
of resolving the story. In 'Worms of the Earth' with Bran Mak

Morn, Howard has to destroy the evil Romans, but he makes creatures come up from underground to do it. Until then, it's a terrific story."

Although he received a co-writing credit, what ended up on screen was a long way from what Oliver Stone (who was also originally supposed to have co-directed with Joe Alves) had envisioned in his original, much more ambitious script.

"Milius had no real interest in collaboration," Stone later recalled. "He took what he wanted from my script, characters and sets, and made it into a strange hybrid of a spaghetti Western and a sword and sandals saga using techniques from his Cinecitta cost-cutting days.

"What is great in Howard's novels is that Conan passes from the stage of peasant to that of a king. A young peasant gains his royalty through a series of tests and marries one of the most beautiful society women."

Despite Oliver Stone's disappointment, the film was a huge success at the box office and led to *The Adventures of Conan: A Sword and Sorcery Spectacular*, a live-action show that ran from 1983–93 at Universal Studios, Hollywood. Produced at a cost of $5 million, the twenty-minute performance featured an eighteen-foot-tall animatronic dragon that breathed fire and a music score composed by Basil Poledouris.

Schwarzenegger returned to the screen in 1984 for *Conan the Destroyer* for veteran director Richard Fleischer. This time Sarah Douglas' treacherous Queen Taramis sent Conan and his companions on a quest for a magical key to unlock the secret of a mystical horn. Filmed on a lower budget in Mexico, this pulpy sequel was slightly more faithful to the spirit of Howard's characters, probably because it was based on a story by comic-book writers Roy Thomas and Gerry Conway.

Schwarzenegger also portrayed Conan-like warrior "Kalidor" in Fleischer's woeful *Red Sonja* (1985), which starred Brigitte

Nielsen as the eponymous swordswoman in a film that barely had any connection to Howard's work.

John Nicolella's *Kull the Conqueror* (1997) featured Kevin Sorbo (TV's "Hercules") as the king of Valusia, who set out to stop Tia Carrere's resurrected witch-queen from using her army of demons to take over the world. The film was apparently derived from a 1991 script for the third Conan film, *Conan the Conquerer*, that was a loose adaptation of 'The Hour of the Dragon'. It had to be abandoned when Arnold Schwarzenegger refused to reprise his role.

Towards the end of 2000, it was announced that Marvel Comics' Stan Lee had purchased the film rights to Conan. However, the project became stalled when Lee's company suspended operations less than three months later, after bridge financing fell through. An attempt by Wachowski brothers Larry and Andy (*The Matrix*, etc.) to develop a movie entitled *King Conan* for Warner Bros., with John Milius once again attached to write and direct, also collapsed in early 2004 over creative differences.

Universal Pictures announced in 2008 that actor Peter Berg would be directing a movie of *Bran Mak Morn* from a screenplay by TV writer John Romano, but nothing ever came of that either.

In an attempt to create a franchise based around another of Robert E. Howard's characters, British actor James Purefoy starred in *Solomon Kane* (2009), in which the eponymous sword-wielding Puritan sought redemption by saving a young girl (Rachel Hurd-Wood) from a sorcerer's murderous cult. Scripted and directed by Michael J. Bassett, the $40 million origin movie proved a disappointment at the box office and plans for a trilogy were scrapped.

Having previously expanded some of Howard's Solomon Kane fragments back in the late 1970s, at least Ramsey Campbell was chosen to write the tie-in film novelisation.

In 2011, Jason Momoa was cast as the mighty Cimmerian in Marcus Nispel's $90 million reboot *Conan the Barbarian*, which retold the barbarian warrior's origin as he sought revenge on the evil warlord (Stephen Lang) who attacked his village and murdered his father (Ron Perlman) when he was just a boy. Unfortunately, although Momoa was fine in the title role, the film flopped at the box office, grossing just $48 million worldwide, and any thoughts about a sequel were quickly abandoned.

"I've been a part of a lot of things that really sucked," recalled Momoa for *British GQ* in 2022, "and movies where it's out of your hands. *Conan* was one of them. It's one of the best experiences I had and it [was] taken over and turned into a big pile of shit."

Director Marcus Nispel agreed with his leading actor: "As a filmmaker in this system you are a dog on many leashes. Trying to get *Conan* done under those circumstances was the worst experience that I had and I was as unhappy with the result."

It was announced in 2012 that *The Legend of Conan* would star Arnold Schwarzenegger, who had played Conan in the original *Conan the Barbarian*. However, this direct sequel to the 1982 movie ran into numerous creative issues and was eventually cancelled five years later.

Robert E. Howard was apparently not even credited on Mindscape International's 1991 *Conan*, the first of many video games based on the character, nor on the 1992–93 syndicated children's cartoon series *Conan the Adventurer*, in which the brawny barbarian (voiced by Michael Donovan) and his comrades set out to undo the spell of living stone cast upon Conan's family by driving the evil serpent men back into another dimension.

Conan and the Young Warriors (1994) was a juvenile spin-off Saturday morning cartoon series on CBS-TV which featured Philip Maurice Hayes as the voice of its barbarian hero.

German weightlifter Ralph Moeller took over the role for the 1997–98 live-action television series *Conan* (aka *Conan the*

Adventurer), produced by Brian Yuzna. The pilot film, *The Heart of the Elephant*, was loosely based on Howard's story 'The Tower of the Elephant' and featured a bizarre computer-created image of the late Richard Burton as the Cimmerian god Crom.

Even more unexpected was Dan Ireland's little 1996 independent film *The Whole Wide World*, based on Novalyne Price Ellis' book *One Who Walked Alone*. Filmed on location in Texas, René Zellweger portrayed the young schoolteacher who befriended eccentric pulp magazine writer Robert E. Howard, played by Vincent D'Onofrio. It is difficult to imagine a more perfect film biography of Howard's final years.

"I know Robert E. Howard probably turned over in his grave fifteen times when *Conan the Barbarian* came out," said Ireland, who died in 2016, "because it's just so bad compared to what it could have been. He was so rich in his vivid portrayal of the worlds, that not to take advantage of that and use that, it was a crime. And I watched it a couple of times—it was hard to watch, but it was important for me to watch it. And I just finally realised I'm going to get much more from just picking up Howard's work and reading it. And I did."

Unlike H.P. Lovecraft, or even Robert E. Howard, there have been precious few media adaptations of Clark Ashton Smith's work.

The third and final season of the anthology television series *Rod Serling's Night Gallery* premiered on NBC-TV on September 24, 1972 with an adaptation of Smith's 'The Return of the Sorcerer'. Directed by Jeannot Szwarc and starring Vincent Price and Bill Bixby, the half-hour show was about a dismembered murder victim who returns from the grave to demand, literally, an eye for an eye. Smith himself said about the story, written in 1931 and published the same year in *Strange Tales*, that it needed "some additional atmospheric development".

Italian director Lucio Fulci included elements from both

Lovecraft and Smith's fiction in his movies *City of the Living Dead* (aka *La paura nella citta dei morti viventi/The Gates of Hell*, 1980) and *The Beyond* (aka *E tu vivrai nel terrore…l'aldila/Seven Doors to Death*, 1981), notably Smith's eldritch volume *The Book of Eibon*.

The six-part anthology film *The Theatre Bizarre* (2011) included director Richard Stanley's co-scripted adaptation of Smith's story 'Mother of Toads' from *Weird Tales* (July, 1938), and in 2019 Woodruff Laputka made a short film from the author's story 'The Last Incantation', which was also originally published in *Weird Tales* (June, 1930).

XXXII

"Lovecraft's particular style is very insidious. It
worms into your brain and stays with you, it instills
a feeling of cosmic dread that's hard to shake."

—Hans Rodionoff

IN THE EARLY 1950s, the controversial EC horror comics line
published a number of stories that, probably due to copyright
restrictions, did not credit H.P. Lovecraft as the source material,
yet still appeared to be unauthorised adaptations of his work.

Amongst the more obvious strips inspired by Lovecraft's
fiction were 'Experiment...in Death" (aka 'Herbert West—
Reanimator', *Weird Science* #12, May 1950), 'Fitting Punishment'
(aka 'In the Vault', *Vault of Horror* #16, December 1950) and 'Baby,
It's Cold Inside' (aka 'Cool Air', *Vault of Horror* #17, February
1951), while other tales mentioned the *Necronomicon* ('The Black
Arts' in *Weird Fantasy* #14, July 1950) and "Cthulhu" ('Who
Doughnut?' in *Vault of Horror* #30, April 1953).

For the following two decades, Warren Publishing was a
successful successor to the old EC comics, and their *Creepy* title
featured two official Lovecraft adaptations: 'The Rats in the Walls'
(#21, July 1968) and 'Cool Air' (#113, November 1979).
Meanwhile, the thirteenth issue of Warren's companion title *Eerie*
(February, 1968) reprinted Russ Jones' graphic version of
'Wentworth's Day'. Adapted from the H.P. Lovecraft and August

Derleth story in *The Survivor and Others*, it was originally published in the paperback collection *Christopher Lee's Treasury of Terror* (1966).

Although both EC and Warren were published outside the Comics Code Authority, Marvel Comics' horror titles of the early 1970s were restricted by what they could show. However, that did not stop them adapting such Lovecraft tales as 'The Terrible Old Man!' (*Tower of Shadows* #3, January 1970), 'The Music from Beyond' (aka 'The Music of Erich Zann', *Chamber of Darkness* #5, June 1970), 'Pickman's Model' (*Tower of Shadows* #9, January 1971) and 'The Haunter of the Dark!' (*Journey Into Mystery* #4, April 1971).

A number of these strips were later reprinted in Marvel's 1975 graphic magazine *Masters of Terror*, while Robert Bloch's Cthulhu Mythos stories 'The Shambler from the Stars' and 'The Shadow from the Steeple' appeared in *Journey Into Mystery* #3 (February, 1973) and #5 (June, 1973), respectively.

West Coast "underground" publisher Last Gasp designated the fourth edition of its "adults only" *Skull Comics* (1972) a special Arkham House and H.P. Lovecraft issue and dedicated it to August Derleth ("for his life-long interest in the medium of the comic strip and his encouragement to us in this special project"). It included black-and-white adaptations of 'The Hound', 'Cool Air' and 'Pickman's Model', along with original material.

The following issue contained graphic versions of 'The Rats in the Walls' and the poem 'To a Dreamer', along with 'The Shadow from the Abyss', an original tale inspired by Lovecraft's work.

The October 1976 issue of *Heavy Metal* magazine was also an H.P. Lovecraft special. As well as a photo-illustration cover by J.K. Potter, it included an adaptation of 'The Dunwich Horror'. P. Craig Russell adapted 'From Beyond' for the May 1994 issue of *Heavy Metal*, while a coloured version of Richard Corben's 'The Rats in the Walls' from *Skull Comics* #5 was featured in the March 1999 edition.

Dell comics had released a tie-in to the American International movie *Die, Monster, Die!* in March 1966, and from 1991–92 Adventure Comics published two three-issue series of comic books based on the 1985 movie *Re-Animator*. From the same imprint, the four issues of *H.P. Lovecraft: The Master of Horror!* (1991–92) contained adaptations of 'The Lurking Fear', 'Beyond the Wall of Sleep', 'The Tomb' and 'The Alchemist'.

Around the same time, Malibu issued the one-off *Re-Animator: Tales of Herbert West* (1991) with Lovecraft's text illustrated in black-and-white, while the ten-issue *The Worlds of H.P. Lovecraft* (1993–98) series from Caliber Comics/Tome Press included 'Arthur Jermyn', 'The Music of Erich Zann', 'The Picture in the House', 'Dagon' (two volumes), 'The Statement of Randolph Carter', 'The Tomb', 'The Alchemist', 'The Lurking Fear' and 'Beyond the Wall of Sleep'.

The Cosmical Horror of H.P. Lovecraft: A Pictorial Anthology was published in 1991 with text in Italian, French and English. It included artwork by Virgil Finlay, Hannes Bok, H.R. Giger, Bernie Wrightson, Richard Corben, Tim White, Guido Buzzelli, Druillet and others.

H.P. Lovecraft's Cthulhu from Millenium adapted 'The Whisperer in Darkness' (1991–92) and 'The Festival' (1994) over three issues apiece. Written and illustrated by Jason Thompson, Mock Man Press published *H.P. Lovecraft's The Dream-Quest of Unknown Kadath* (1997–99). The five-issue series was issued as an animated film in 2004, limited to 1,000 numbered DVD copies.

"Upon first reading 'The Dream-Quest of Unknown Kadath', I knew I'd found a work which was the greatest of H.P. Lovecraft's early dream stories," explained Thompson, "the purest of his sometimes hateful or jaded philosophy, and which was crowded with the most unique imagery in any fantasy novel of the 20th century.

"From the sleeping village of Ulthar to the allegorical islands of the Southern Sea, from the garden lands beside the Skai to Kadath itself, Lovecraft had created a world that yearned to be experienced—or at least seen. Kadath is an unrevised, flawed work, but this only adds to its mythical feeling; there are many fantasy novels with superior plots, but in terms of visual invention, nothing can touch 'Kadath.'"

H.P. Lovecraft's *The Haunter of the Dark and Other Grotesque Visions* (1999) was published by Oneiros Books in trade paperback format. It collected numerous black-and-white illustrations and three comic-strip adaptations of Lovecraft's stories by British artist John Coulthart, with an introduction by Alan Moore.

Published by Cross Plains Comics in July 2000, writer Roy Thomas and Spanish artist Esteban Maroto adapted 'The Call of Cthulhu', 'The Festival' and 'The Nameless City' for *H.P. Lovecraft's The Call of Cthulhu*.

Graphic Classics: H.P. Lovecraft (2002) was the fourth volume in the series from Eureka Productions adapting the work of classic authors to comic strip format. The 144-page trade paperback included versions of 'Herbert West—Reanimator', 'The Shadow Out of Time', 'The Cats of Ulthar', 'The Terrible Old Man', 'The Dream-Quest of Unknown Kadath', 'The Outsider' and 'Fungi from Yuggoth', along with other material. The impressive line-up of contributors included Richard Corben, Rick Geary, Matt Howarth, Tom Sutton, Stephen Hickman, John Coulthart, Allen Koszowski, S. Clay Wilson and Gahan Wilson. A second, later printing added 'The Shadow Over Innsmouth', 'Dreams in the Witch-House' and the Lovecraft comedy 'Sweet Ermengarde'.

Featuring an introduction by film director John Carpenter, *Lovecraft* (2004) was a heavily fictionalised biography of Howard Phillips Lovecraft. An original hardcover graphic novel from DC Comics/Vertigo, it was penned by scriptwriter Hans Rodionoff with Keith Giffen and painted by Argentine artist Enriqué Breccia.

"Lovecraft's particular style is very insidious," observed

Rodionoff, who based the book on an unproduced screenplay. "It worms into your brain and stays with you, it instills a feeling of cosmic dread that's hard to shake."

Fall of Cthulhu was an epic comic book series from Boom! Studios (2007–08), created by writer Michael Alan Nelson. Inspired by Lovecraft's concepts, it postulated that 'The Call of Cthulhu' could be happening again in the present day. The initial run of fifteen issues was followed by a further four mini-series.

In 2010, *At the Mountains of Madness* was adapted into a graphic novel by I.N.J. Culbard and published by SelfMadeHero as part of their Eye Classics line. Mike Mignola—whose own *Hellboy* series was greatly influenced by Lovecraft—created an alternate world Batman/Cthulhu mash-up in the 2015 graphic novel *The Doom That Came to Gotham* from DC Comics, while *The Call of Cthulhu: A Mystery in Three Parts* from Flesk Publications featured more than 100 pencil drawings by Gary Gianni.

To date there have litererally been hundreds of adaptions of H.P. Lovecraft's stories in graphic form, while his relatively small body of fiction continues to influence many more comic creators to this day.

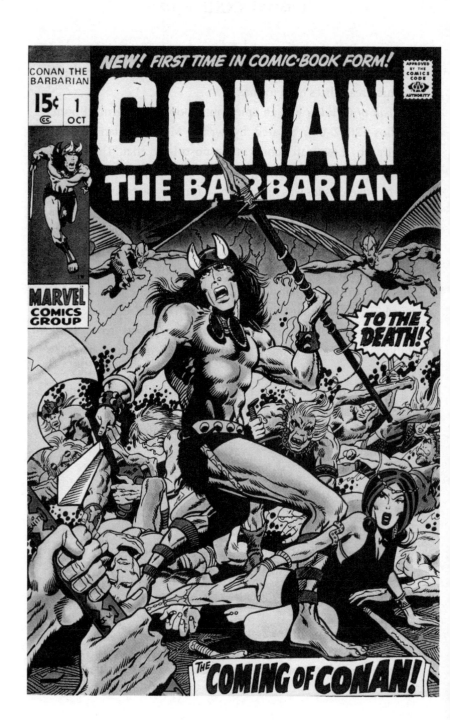

XXXIII

"I liked to tie Conan and Kull together—even to the
point of intimating that the Cimmerian might be a
linear descendent of the Atlantean."

—Roy Thomas

J UST AS EC Comics unofficially used H.P. Lovecraft's stories as
the basis for some of its comic strips, so another 1950s horror
comic also "borrowed" its plot from Robert E. Howard's work, with
'Skulls of Doom' in Four Star Publications' *Voodoo* #12 (November,
1953) being loosely based on the author's 1933 *Weird Tales* story
'Old Garfield's Heart'.

La reina de la Costa Negra was an unlicensed Mexican comics
adaptation of Howard's 1934 *Weird Tales* story 'Queen of the Black
Coast', featuring the female pirate Bêlit and a *blond* Conan. The
first version was originally serialised in Corporacion Editorial
Mexicana's *Cuentos de Abuelito* (Grandpa's Stories, 1952–53). A
new serialisation ran in its own publication from Ediciones
Mexicanas Asociadas in 1958–59, while the story was adapted yet
again by Ediciones Joma in the mid-1960s, and these were
reprinted in a slightly larger format in 2008.

In October 1970, having failed to secure the rights to Lin
Carter's sword and sorcery character Thongor of Lemuria, Marvel
Comics Group launched its hugely successful *Conan the Barbarian*
title, written by Roy Thomas and initially illustrated by artist Barry
(Windsor-) Smith.

229

"One night I passed a copy of the latest Conan paperback: *Conan of Cimmeria*," recalled Thomas some years later. "I glanced at L. Sprague de Camp's introduction therein, and saw the name and even address of 'the literary agent for the Robert E. Howard estate', one Glenn Lord. On a whim I sent Glenn a letter (it was too complicated at Marvel to get reimbursed for phone calls back then)—offering him the grandiloquent sum of $200 per issue for the rights for Marvel to publish a *Conan* comic book. I explained politely that I had no real leeway for negotiations, but that such a comic might give the hero a whole new audience and thus be worthwhile for the estate. Amazingly, Glenn concurred—and we were in business.

"For the comic's title I suggested *Conan the Barbarian*—a phrase never precisely used, word for word, in any of the two dozen published REH tales—because that had been the title of one of the Gnome hardcovers and had thus not been used as the name of one of the newer paperbacks with which readers were far more familiar."

Many issues of the comic adapted or were based on Howard's original stories, and there was even a two-issue crossover with Michael Moorcock's Elric of Melniboné, while a Tarzan-type character named Amra was introduced later. In May 1971, Marvel launched another series of Conan adaptations by Thomas in *Savage Tales*. *Conan the Barbarian King-Size* appeared in 1973, and it was followed over the years by such titles as *The Savage Sword of Conan*, *King Conan*, *Conan the Destroyer* and *The Conan Saga*.

As Roy Thomas explained, Marvel's *Conan* magazines contained "a combination of three types of tales: the occasional one based on an actual Robert E. Howard Conan saga (where it fit in chronologically), original stories, and adaptations of a non-Conan effort by REH into a comics adventure (along the lines of L. Sprague de Camp's prose efforts of the same type)."

Following the moderately successful debut of its *Conan the*

Barbarian title the previous year, Marvel Comics introduced readers in March 1971 to Kull in *Creatures on the Loose!* #10. Thomas wrote the story 'Skull in the Silence', while Berni Wrightson supplied the artwork.

Three months later, the ever-busy Thomas launched *Kull the Conqueror* with an adaptation of Howard's story 'Exile of Atlantis' and the first chapter of 'The Shadow Kingdom'. Ross Andru and Wally Wood provided the art.

"Kull lived thousands of years before Conan," Roy Thomas revealed, "but although REH never did so, I liked to tie Conan and Kull together—even to the point of intimating that the Cimmerian might be a linear descendent of the Atlantean."

After ten issues, the title of the comic was changed to *Kull the Destroyer* in 1973 with an adaptation of 'By This Axe I Rule!' by Thomas, who had also contributed an original Kull story, 'The Forbidden Swamp', to the April 1972 issue of *Monsters on the Prowl*.

In the early 1970s, Marvel also adapted three of Howard's stand-alone horror stories into comics form. 'Dig Me No Grave' appeared in *Journey Into Mystery* #1 (October, 1972) scripted by Roy Thomas with art by Gil Kane and Ton Palmer. 'The Monster from the Mound' (based on 'The Horror from the Mound') was adapted by Gardner Fox for *Chamber of Chills* #2 (January, 1973), while Thomas scripted 'The Thing on the Roof!' in *Chamber of Chills* #3 (March, 1973). Both the latter strips were illustrated by Frank Brunner.

Kull continued to appear in Marvel's *Kull and the Barbarians* and various *Conan* titles. In 1981, the character even met the astral spirit of Spider-Man, sent back in time by Doctor Strange, in *Marvel Team-Up* #112. That same year, 'Demon in a Silvered Glass' was a loose adaptation by Doug Moench of 'The Mirrors of Tuzun Thune' in *Bizarre Adventures* #26.

Roy Thomas also adapted the Solomon Kane story 'Skulls in the Stars' for the first issue of Marvel Comics' *Monsters Unleashed* in 1973, and in October the same year he contributed an original Kane strip, 'Castle of the Undead', to the third issue of Marvel's *Dracula Lives!*

Originally published in the February 1934 issue of *Weird Tales*, Howard's story about James Allison, 'The Valley of the Worm', was adapted into comic form by Roy Thomas and Gerry Conway for the third issue of Marvel's *Supernatural Thrillers* (April, 1973), with artwork by Gil Kane and Ernie Chua. Three years later it became the basis of another graphic adaptation, *Bloodstar*, from Morning Star Press. Artist Richard Corben and fantasy writer John Jakes set their version of the tale in a post-apocalyptic future.

Interestingly, when the same strip was reprinted in the late 1970s, it was rewritten by John Pocsik, who had previously completed Howard's Solomon Kane story 'The Blue Flame of Vengeance' for August Derleth's anthology *Over the Edge*.

Roy Thomas also adapted Howard's 'The Hills of the Dead' for two issues of *Kull and the Barbarians* in 1975 and 'Red Shadows' over two issues of *Marvel Premiere Featuring The Mark of Kane* in 1976–77. Don Glut contributed a version of 'The Footfalls Within' to the Summer 1979 issue of *Marvel Preview*.

In 1980–81, 'Almuric' was adapted by Thomas over four issues of Marvel's prestige publication, *Epic Illustrated*. Originally intended to appear in *Marvel Premiere* under the title 'Warrior of the Lost Planet', this truncated version of the short novel was illustrated by Tim Conrad.

After appearing in back-up stories in *The Savage Sword of Conan* (including two versions of the poem 'Solomon Kane's Homecoming'), Howard's hero finally got his own title from Marvel with the six-issue mini-series *The Sword of Solomon Kane* in 1985–86.

Kull: The Vale of the Shadow was a graphic novel by Alan Zelenetz that was published by Marvel in 1989, and in 2006 Dark Horse Comics purchased the rights to the character, two years later launching *Kull* with a four-part adaptation by Arvid Nelson of 'The Shadow Kingdom'.

Also in 2008, Dark Horse released a new five-issue adaptation of 'The Castle of the Devil' in *Solomon Kane*, scripted by Scott Allie. The first issue featured variant covers by John Cassaday and Joe Kubert. It was followed by two more mini-series, 'Death's Black Riders' (2010) and yet another graphic version of 'Red Shadows' (2011).

Dark Horse also published *Conan the Cimmerian* (2008–10), while Howard's story 'The Mirrors of Tuzun Thune' formed the basis for IDW Publishing's *Kull Eternal* in 2017, which reimagined the character in a contemporary setting.

Although, unlike Conan, Solomon Kane and Kull, Bran Mak Morn never got his own title from Marvel Comics, the character did turn up in several issues of *The Savage Sword of Conan*, including adaptations of Howard's 'Men of the Shadows' and 'Worms of the Earth', both scripted by the ubiquitous Roy Thomas.

"I genuinely liked working with REH's prose," Thomas explained, "putting more of it out there for readers to appreciate."

In 2000, Cross Plains Comics/Wandering Star reissued Roy Thomas' adaptation of *Worms of the Earth* in trade paperback with a host of extra features, including interviews, essays and additional artwork by Gary Gianni, Mark Schultz and Jim and Ruth Keegan.

Starting in 2003, Dark Horse Books began republishing Marvel's *Conan* adaptations as omnibus graphic novel collections under the title *The Chronicles of Conan*. Roy Thomas contributed a series of fascinating Afterwords that charted his history with the character.

Despite being one of the "Big Three" from *Weird Tales*, Clark Ashton Smith's work has not been adapted for the graphic medium anywhere near as much as that of his colleagues Robert E. Howard or H.P. Lovecraft.

That said, as happened to both his friends, Smith's work was also occasionally swiped by the horror comics of the 1950s.

'Terror on the Moors!' in EC Comics' *Vault of Horror* #17 (February–March, 1951) was an "unofficial" adaptation by Johnny Craig of Smith's story 'The Nameless Offspring' from the June 1932 issue of *Strange Tales*.

Another of the author's stories from that pulp magazine, 'The Return of the Sorcerer', formed the basis for 'The Corpse That Wouldn't Die!' with art by Jack Cole in the second issue of *Web of Evil* (January, 1953).

'The Ninth Skeleton' was Smith's first fiction appearance in *Weird Tales* (September, 1928), and it was adapted by Tom Yeates for *Third Rail Magazine* #1 (June 1981), before being reprinted eight years later in the first issue of *Asylum*.

During the 1990s, a number of Clark Ashton Smith's stories were adapted into Conan strips for Marvel, all scripted by Roy Thomas. The Hyperborea tale 'The Weird of Avoosl Wuthoqquan' was "freely adapted" for *Conan the Adventurer* #8 (January, 1995) with art by John Watkiss, while 'The Abominations of Yondo' was illustrated by Rafael Kayanan and John Floyd in *Conan the Adventurer* #12 (May, 1995) and was "inspired" by the author's prose-poem in the *Overland Monthly* (April, 1926). Another story, 'The Inquisitors of Ong' in *Conan the Adventurer* #11 (April, 1995), was "suggested by a tale by Clark Ashton Smith".

The "Zothique" tale 'Necromancy in Naat' from *Weird Tales* (July, 1936) became 'The Necromancers of Na'at' in *Conan the Savage* #10 (May, 1996) with art by John and Stephanie Buscema. It was somewhat confusingly reworked as a sequel to L. Sprague DeCamp and Lin Carter's 1968 novel *Conan of the Isles*.

Smith's 'The Seed from the Sepulcher' in *Heavy Metal* #3 (July, 1999) was adapted and drawn by Richard Corben from its original appearance in *Weird Tales* (October, 1933). 'The Vaults of Yoh-Vombis' was a science fiction/horror story from the May 1932 issue of that pulp which Corben also adapted and illustrated for *DenSaga* #2 (1993), and he followed it up in *DenSaga* #3 (1993) with another adaptation of 'The Return of the Sorcerer'.

Mock Man Press' *Clark Ashton Smith's Hyperborea* (2004) contained the 1931 *Weird Tales* story 'The Tale of Satampra Zeiros', adapted and illustrated by Jason Thompson. The story introduced the author's own loathsome addition to the Cthulhu Mythos, the dark god Tsathoggua. The twenty-page graphic novel also included a map of Hyperborea and additional artwork by tattooist Adam Burns.

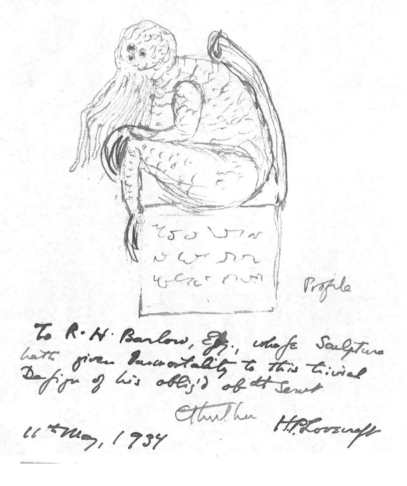

CALL of CTHULHU

Fantasy Role-Playing in the Worlds of H. P. Lovecraft

WINNER
Best Role-Playing
Game
H.G. WELLS AWARD
STRATEGISTS CLUB
AWARD
GAME DESIGNERS'
GUILD SELECT
AWARD

SANDY PETERSEN

Yurek Chodak, Tadashi Ehara, Harry
Henderson, Charlie Krank, Steve Perrin,
Greg Stafford, Anders Swenson, Lynn
Willis. Gene Day illus.

by permission of
ARKHAM HOUSE

CHAOSIUM
INC.

XXXIV

"If you want a game in which the emphasis is far
more cerebral, and more dangerous, and in which
the enemies pose an existential threat—there is only
Call of Cthulhu."

—Sandy Petersen

FOLLOWING AN ABORTED attempt by games manu-
facturer TSR, Inc. in the early 1980s to incorporate H.P.
Lovecraft's pantheon of elder gods into one of its Dungeons &
Dragons scenarios, Chaosium released *The Call of Cthulhu: Horror
Role-playing in the Worlds of H.P. Lovecraft* in 1981. Thanks to the
detailed background material derived from its source material, the
award-winning game became a huge success and, as with the
author's original stories, spawned a whole industry of spin-off
supplements, an adventure board game (*Arkham Horror*), a live-
action game (*Cthulhu Live*), collectible card games (*Mythos* and
Call of Cthulhu) and numerous tie-in books.

"If you want a game in which you have the same old steroid-
pumped champions confronting the baddies, every other RPG can
provide this," explained original designer Sandy Petersen. "But if
you want a game in which the emphasis is far more cerebral, and
more dangerous, and in which the enemies pose an existential
threat—there is only *Call of Cthulhu*."

Infocom's *The Lurking Horror* (1987) was an interactive game
written by Dave Lebling and inspired by Lovecraft's fiction,

including the Cthulhu Mythos, as was the 1992 video game *Alone in the Dark* (even down to specific names and titles).

Developed by Be Top and published by I'Max in Japan in 1995, *Innsmouth no Yakata* was a first-person horror video game loosely based on the Lovecraft story, while *Call of Cthulhu: Dark Corners of the Earth* was a first-person survival game also inspired by 'The Shadow Over Innsmouth'. Developed by Britain's Headfirst Productions, it was released by Bethesda Softworks and 2K Games in 2006.

The first Conan computer game was *Conan: Hall of Volta* (1984), produced by Datasoft. This was followed in 1991 by Mindscape's *Conan: The Mysteries of Time* and Synergistic Software's *Conan: The Cimmerian* the same year.

Published by TSR in 1985, *Conan Role-Playing Game* was a boxed set designed for players aged ten years and up, while *Conan: The Roleplaying Game* was an RPG created by Mongoose Publishing in 2004. Fantasy Flight Games released the strategy board game *Age of Conan* in 2009, which depicted warfare between the Hyborian nations, and the British game company Modiphius Entertainment's *Conan: Adventures in an Age Undreamed Of* was a pen-and-paper role-playing game funded through Kickstarter and released in 2017.

Based on Pinnacle Entertainment Group's "Savage Worlds" game system, *Savage World of Solomon Kane* was written by Paul Wade-Williams and Shane Lacy Hensley and released in 2007, while Keith Herber's scenario *Spawn of Tsathoggua* was part of Chaosium's "Call of Cthulhu" series of RPG adventures and inspired by the work of Clark Ashton Smith.

Illustrated by D.L. Hutchinson, *The Lovecraft Tarot* was issued by Mythos Books in 1998, and the *Conan Collectible Card Game* designed by Jason Robinette was released by Comic Images in 2006.

In recent years, Lovecraft fans could choose between collectible action figure sets featuring Dagon and Cthulhu, T-shirts emblazoned with "Collect Call of Cthulhu" or "Pokéthulu" designs and, perhaps most disconcerting of all, a cute and cuddly Baby Shoggoth plush or various Cthulhu soft dolls with poseable wings and floppy tentacles.

Fans of Robert E. Howard's Conan were offered everything from limited-edition mini-busts of the mighty Cimmerian himself, Valeria (the swordswoman from 'Red Nails') and sorcerer Thoth-Amon, to a Conan lunch box featuring artwork by Barry Windsor-Smith and a Conan Atlantean Sword made from folded Damascus steel.

Tony Cipriano sculpted a King Kull mini-bust that was part of "The Savage Sword Collection" and limited to 1,200 pieces, while designer Gary Gianni and sculptor Randy Bowen's cold-cast bronze statue of Solomon Kane was issued in a limited edition of only 550 pieces.

Red·Shadows·
By·ROBERT·E·HOWARD·

"He sheathed his dagger to the hilt in the Rat's back."

XXXV

"Personally I should not care for immortality in the least."

—H.P. Lovecraft

PERHAPS THE TRAGEDY of Clark Ashton Smith is that, unlike his more famous contemporaries, Lovecraft and Howard, he actually lived to see his work republished and acclaimed. Whereas, as Robert Bloch explained, "The sheer abundance of data and hypotheses lends glamour to both Lovecraft's and Howard's reputations", Smith survived into his late sixties and although he received a margin of the critical praise and attention his work deserved, a mass readership and the commensurate commercial rewards always eluded him.

"The glory that feeds on gossip is denied him and he remains a shy, quiet enigma," Bloch revealed; "we are aware of his presence as a poet but the man himself remains a shadow".

Despite being acclaimed a genius while still a teenager, the man who cast that shadow may have yet to attain the cult status of his two friends. Yet his unique prose and poetry remain with us as a testament to his lasting genius and imagination.

As Ray Bradbury observed: "Smith always seemed, to me anyway, a special writer for special tastes; his fame was lonely."

Robert E. Howard is best remembered for his stories about

Conan of Cimmeria. Often written for less than a cent per word and published in disposable magazines printed on cheap pulp paper, his tales about the mighty barbarian have remained with us over the decades. Today, through films, television and comic books, Howard's name is more widely known than it ever was during his lifetime. Conan has outlived his creator and, perhaps with the exception of Edgar Rice Burroughs' Tarzan, is possibly the best-known character in modern fantasy fiction.

However, Howard was also a prolific writer of fantasy, horror, historical adventure, Westerns, detective, sports stories, true confessions and other genre fiction. During his tragically short career, he created a number of other memorable characters and published numerous short stories that, over the years, have been somewhat eclipsed by the justifiably acclaimed exploits of his Hyborian hero.

At his best, Robert E. Howard could sweep the reader away on a red tide of bloodlust to lost cities, unexplored jungles and savage pirate galleons, where all a brave man needed was a sharp sword in his hand and a beautiful woman by his side to face whatever hideous horror or supernatural menace confronted him.

Artist Mark Schultz noted: "Howard's fantasies are soaked through with Howard. His writing is unmistakenly his. He transcends the genre he created, giving us something of himself, and so has remained unmatched in storytelling drive and skill at evoking atmosphere, mayhem and anguish."

Unfortunately, in recent years Robert E. Howard's reputation has been somewhat tarnished by acusations of racism in his life, letters and fiction. It has also been pointed out that although the racism of his day is present and accounted for in some of his stories, such as the zombie tale 'Black Canaan' (*Weird Tales*, June 1936), it is also often subverted and undermined in others as well (as in some of the Conan stories).

As his friend H.P. Lovecraft accurately observed: "It is hard to describe precisely what made Mr. Howard's stories stand out so sharply; but the real secret is that he himself is in every one of them... He was greater than any profit-making policy he could adopt—for even when he outwardly made concessions to Mammon-guided editors and commercial critics, he had an internal force and sincerity which broke through the surface and put the imprint of his personality on everything he wrote. Before he concluded with it, it always took on some tinge of vitality and reality in spite of popular editorial policy—always drew something from his own experience and knowledge of life instead of from the sterile herbarium of desiccated pulpish standby. Not only did he excel in pictures of strife and slaughter, but he was almost alone in his ability to create real emotions of spectral fear and dread suspense. No author—even in the humblest fields—can truly excel unless he takes his work very seriously; and Mr. Howard did just that even in cases where he consciously thought he did not."

For the discerning reader of heroic fantasy fiction, Robert E. Howard's talent and tragedy will continue to live on through his fiction and the enduring adventures of his greatest creation, Conan the Cimmerian.

In the decades since his untimely death at the age of forty-six years and seven months, H.P. Lovecraft and his works have become a marketing brand that is recognised all over the world. In a manner that he could never have imagined during his lifetime, while eking out a living revising other writers' manuscripts and selling the occasional story to the pulp magazines, the author has even eclipsed his literary hero Edgar Allan Poe, and is now widely regarded as the pre-eminent American horror writer of all time.

All of his fiction continues to be available in hardcover and paperback editions, and anthology editors still draw extensively upon his relatively small cadre of stories. His writings continue to sell millions of copies throughout the world, and have been translated into every major language. Today, there are numerous web sites and blogs devoted to the author and his work.

"H.P. Lovecraft is not only the essential link between Edgar Allan Poe and the present day," observed Neil Gaiman, "he has become an almost unimaginably influential force throughout the whole of our popular culture."

In December 2006, Sotheby's auction house sold a signed manuscript of 'The Shunned House' for $45,000.00. An autographed manuscript of 'Under the Pyramids' achieved $24,000.00 and, even more staggering, a group of fifty letters by Lovecraft sold to an American dealer for a record $48,000.00. A total of twenty lots realised $203,400.00.

"Personally I should not care for immortality in the least," Lovecraft wrote in 1921, and yet that is exactly what this Gentleman of Providence has achieved through his work, more than eighty-five years after he died in relative obscurity.

"It is not for any of Lovecraft's friends to give an estimate of any value as to his position in the literature of the macabre and of pure imagination," wrote W. Paul Cook. "Such an estimate from a friend will be both too high and too low. Possibly he will hold a permanent position more because of his influence than for what he actually wrote. His invention of a completely new out-of-space mythology which has been extensively adopted and used by other writers may be his final bid for lasting fame."

Regrettably, despite his continued influence on horror fiction and film, of all the "Big Three" from *Weird Tales* it is H.P. Lovecraft's reputation that has taken the greatest beating in recent years.

Nigerian-American writer Nnedi Okorafor sparked a backlash against the author after she won the World Fantasy Award for Best Novel in 2011. In a blog post soon afterwards, she highlighted a particularly unpleasant poem that Lovecraft had written when he was in his early twenties, expressing her discomfort with the award itself—a stylised bust of Lovecraft created by cartoonist Gahan Wilson and presented at the World Fantasy Convention since its inception in 1975.

This came at the beginning of social media's "cancel culture" movement, and soon people were scrutinising every word the author had written to find examples of his "bigotry", "racism", "anti-Semitism", "homophobia" and "white supremacy" in stories such as 'The Call of Cthulhu', 'The Shadow Over Innsmouth' and 'The Horror at Red Hook'.

There is no doubt that some of those things had always been there as subtext in his fiction, although many supporters continue to argue that the author's views were not considered extreme at the time he was writing. However, as a result of the controversy, Lovecraft became an early casualty of the culture wars when, in 2015, it was announced that, despite holding a ballot amongst the membership, the organisers had already decided that the statuette in his image (nicknamed the "Howard" in honour of *both* Lovecraft and Robert E. Howard) would henceforth be retired.

Perhaps it is best left to his devotee and literary saviour, August Derleth, to sum up Howard Phillips Lovecraft's standing as an author: "Lovecraft was an original in the Gothic tradition," he explained in *H.P.L.: A Memoir*; "he was a skilled writer of supernatural fiction, a master of the macabre who had no peer in the America of his time, and only the fact that in America there is no quality market for the supernatural tale prevented his work from reaching a wider audience. By his own choice he was in his letters, as in his personal existence, an outsider in his time."

From a contemporary perspective, it is probably safe to say that whether he wanted it or not, and despite the controversy that continues to rage around the man and his work today, Howard Philips Lovecraft is no longer the outsider that he once was.

Successive generations of writers have continued to acknowledge their debt to the author's work. "Lovecraft opened the way for me," Stephen King has said, "as he had done for others before me—Robert Bloch, Fritz Leiber and Ray Bradbury among them. The reader would do well to remember that it is his shadow, so long and so gaunt, and his eyes, so dark and puritanical, which overlie almost all of the important horror fiction that has come since."

For these three writers—Howard Phillips Lovecraft, Robert Ervin Howard and Clark Ashton Smith—it has been a long journey, and probably not the journey that any of them could ever have imagined during their lifetimes.

However, it is difficult to imagine any other authors from that period still having such a profound influence on horror and fantasy fiction today. Whether you love them or hate them, these "Weird Tales Boys" continue to cast their long, talented and in some ways tragic shadows over our genre.

May it always remain so.

ABOUT THE AUTHOR

Photo © Mandy Slater

STEPHEN JONES lives in London, England. A Hugo Award nominee, he is the winner of four World Fantasy Awards, three International Horror Guild Awards, five Bram Stoker Awards, twenty-one British Fantasy Awards and a Lifetime Achievement Award from the Horror Writers Association. One of Britain's most acclaimed horror and dark fantasy writers and editors, he has more than 165 books to his credit, including the acclaimed illustrated histories *The Art of Horror, The Art of Horror Movies and The Art of Pulp Horror*, the film books of Neil Gaiman's *Coraline* and *Stardust, The Illustrated Monster Movie Guide* and *The Hellraiser Chronicles*; the non-fiction studies *Horror: 100 Best Books and Horror: Another 100 Best Books* (both with Kim Newman); single-author collections by H. P. Lovecraft, Robert E. Howard, M.R. James, David Case, R. Chetwynd-

Hayes, Basil Copper, Aidan Chambers, Lionel Fanthorpe and Robert Silverberg; anthologies such as *Terrifying Tales to Tell at Night: 10 Scary Stories to Give You Nightmares!* and *The Mammoth Book of Folk Horror*, plus the *Best New Horror, The Alchemy Press Book of the Dead, The Lovecraft Squad* and *Zombie Apocalypse!* series.

You can visit his web site at www.stephenjones-editor.com or follow him on Facebook at "Stephen Jones-Editor".

STEPHEN JONES' MASTERS OF HORROR SERIES

#1   *Basil Copper: A Life in Books*

#2   *Darkness, Mist & Shadow: The Collected Macabre Tales of Basil Copper Basil Copper Volume One*

#3   *Darkness, Mist & Shadow: The Collected Macabre Tales of Basil Copper Basil Copper Volume Two*

#4   *Darkness, Mist & Shadow: The Collected Macabre Tales of Basil Copper Basil Copper Volume Three*

#5   *Pelican Cay & Other Disquieting Tales* by David Case

#6   *Scream Quietly: The Best of Charles L. Grant*

#7   *The Curse of the Fleers* by Basil Copper

#8   *The Complete Adventures of Solar Pons Volume 1* by Basil Copper

#9   *The Complete Adventures of Solar Pons Volume 2* by Basil Copper

#10 *Gaslight, Ghosts & Ghouls: A Centenary Celebration* by R. Chetwynd-Hayes

#11 *Dead Trouble & Other Ghost Stories* by Aidan Chambers

#12 *New Supernatural Stories* by Lionel and Patricia Fanthorpe

#13 *Kong: An Original Screenplay* by Edgar Wallace

#14 *Robert Silverberg's Monsters and Things*

#15 *The Weird Tales Boys: H.P. Lovecraft, Robert E. Howard, Clark Ashton Smith and "The Unique Magazine"* by Stephen Jones